Life
A Mystery Solved

ZIRI DAFRANCHI

WestBow Press
A DIVISION OF THOMAS NELSON
& ZONDERVAN

Copyright © 2016 Ziri Dafranchi.

All rights reserved. No part of this book may be used or reproduced by any means, graphic, electronic, or mechanical, including photocopying, recording, taping or by any information storage retrieval system without the written permission of the author except in the case of brief quotations embodied in critical articles and reviews.

WestBow Press books may be ordered through booksellers or by contacting:

WestBow Press
A Division of Thomas Nelson & Zondervan
1663 Liberty Drive
Bloomington, IN 47403
www.westbowpress.com
1 (866) 928-1240

Because of the dynamic nature of the Internet, any web addresses or links contained in this book may have changed since publication and may no longer be valid. The views expressed in this work are solely those of the author and do not necessarily reflect the views of the publisher, and the publisher hereby disclaims any responsibility for them.

Any people depicted in stock imagery provided by Thinkstock are models, and such images are being used for illustrative purposes only. Certain stock imagery © Thinkstock.

ISBN: 978-1-5127-4391-3 (sc)
ISBN: 978-1-5127-4393-7 (hc)
ISBN: 978-1-5127-4392-0 (e)

Library of Congress Control Number: 2016908649

Print information available on the last page.

WestBow Press rev. date: 6/3/2016

For every one who has, who now, and who will make the journey. For Dad; who turned a corner, and we saw him no more.

Table of Contents

Preface ix

Part 1: The Beginning..1
Chapter 1. Inception 3
Chapter 2. Who am I? 10
Chapter 3. Why am I here? 21

Part 2: The Journey..33
Chapter 4. Where from? Where to ? 35
Chapter 5. Rat race 40
Chapter 6. Mind control 48
Chapter 7. Love and relationships... 60
Chapter 8. Money rules... 76
Chapter 9. Religion 91
Chapter 10. Who exactly is God? 119
Chapter 11. A new me...158
Chapter 12. A brand new world 170

Part 3: The End...179
Chapter 13. A time to die..181
Chapter 14. Goodbye, World 200
Chapter 15. What happens after death?..................................214

Epilogue 223
Bibliography.. 227

Preface

Life : A Mystery Solved is primarily the product of a personal journey; it is the result of various personal reflections and meditations occasioned by that journey. The journey, though still ongoing, at a particular stage took a very significant dimension which resulted in a profound personal transformation: I would eventually begin to gradually understand who I really was (and, effectively, who I was meant to be); which led to my gradually discovering some of the things I might've been created to do (possibly, the things which necessitated my birth in the first place) and both realisations exposed me to a new meaning and significance of life, on a personal level, as well as in general.

Although most of the insights expounded came mainly as a result of various experiences encountered during that particular stage of the journey, which occurred in adulthood — especially between 2012 and 2015 — it would be right to say that all opinions expressed in the book largely have been informed or influenced by the many direct and personal experiences I have been privileged with since my birth.

During the particular stage in reference, which I would later describe as "My Journey to Freedom", I experienced a unique form of mind renewal and also a higher level of spiritual awakening. Consequently, my original perception of life would significantly be altered: I began to see a whole lot of things differently; most things were no longer to me what they used to be. This new level of awareness prompted me to start expressing my new-found realisations in blogs which I shared on social media — notably, Google plus (G+), Facebook and Twitter — and it so happened that the more I wrote the more inspirations I received, which would subsequently lead to more new discoveries. The more I wrote the more I would become further enlightened and the deeper my insights all of which further assisted in broadening my understanding and perception of life. My natural curiosity having been awakened, I was prompted to delve deeper as I sought to know more, especially the truth regarding some long-held personal beliefs and ideologies, based on my upbringing, including those relating to religion. As a result, I began to investigate different issues — as and when prompted — and I began to dig deeper in personal studies while also conducting minor researches where necessary: I sought out various research-based publications — online and offline — in the relevant subject areas; I also resorted to the Holy Bible severally, in search of answers and, where applicable, to crosscheck some findings from other sources. I approached my quest with an open mind; I wanted nothing but the whole truth.

Consequently, I was greatly surprised by some of the things I would later discover which seemed to contradict some of my earlier beliefs, things I had previously believed to be either right or true. In some cases, I was actually shocked when I found out that some of these things were already common knowledge with some members of the public, even though I was only just becoming aware of them, but what really surprised me even more was that such people seemed to be more or less quiet about what they knew, probably having taken it for granted that everyone else was similarly informed as themselves. But not everyone is privy to some of these information and knowledge, at least I wasn't until then. I then reasoned that it was a vital necessity, almost a duty, to make everyone aware of these hidden or obscure truths. As a result, I desired that everyone who already didn't know these things should be adequately informed; I wanted as many people as didn't already know what I now knew to know.

And so, I started writing and blogging.

As a result of the level of interest and activity that some of these rather short blogs generated — in addition to the fact that over time I quickly realised that my blogs, limited by their brevity, lacked the right amount of detail needed to make them more effective as sources of information and new awareness — it subsequently dawned on me that books, instead of various short blogs, would be a better and more effective medium for spreading the awareness I greatly desired and wanted to achieve.

Life: A Mystery Solved is the first of those books and it presents life — i.e. its mortal or natural state — as a journey, which commences at birth and terminates at death. It gives you a panoramic view of life, but more than just presenting you with a pictorial representation it encourages you to be a part of the picture by requiring your active participation in the adventure. It is interactive and it invites you to participate. If you do, you are likely to realise that you are not just part of an audience observing life from a safe distance but instead a key player and the main character in the entire plot. Consequently, you may discover many things about yourself you previously didn't know — possibly because you have never really attempted to consciously understand who you are or why you are — and you may also discover that the life you have lived so far is the one you have, probably unwittingly, chosen; a choice which most likely has been largely influenced by public or societal standards. As your active participation progresses, you are also likely to realise that your life could be better — much better — simply by making some new choices, but this time with you as the main influence.

Life: A Mystery Solved is based on truth: to maximise its benefits, you will have to be sincere with yourself as you participate in the interactions it invites you to partake in. The truth sets free, but only if wholly accepted and diligently applied. Similarly, the book is about **YOU** and no one else: to benefit the most from it, you are encouraged to focus primarily and solely on self; it is aimed at self-discovery through self-assessment. It isn't a guidebook for group exercises rather it is a personal workbook.

Finally, at the core of **Life: A Mystery Solved** is your spiritual existence: although it deals with many other aspects of life, e.g. psychological, mental, emotional, financial, etc., it is rooted firmly on your spiritual being; the human spirit is the hub to which all the other aspects of life are connected; the human spirit is also the driving force of life. Consequently, a supernatural involvement in your participation — in the form of divine assistance — is of utmost necessity if the book is to make any sense to you and if it would benefit you at all. Otherwise, you may become more mystified than enlightened at the end of the journey, and might be left with more questions than answers.

Now, brace yourself as you embark on what I hope would be a very interesting and adventurous journey.

I wish you a pleasant journey.

Part One
The Beginning

In the beginning God created the heaven and the earth.

Genesis 1:1 (KJV)

Chapter 1

Inception

Through medical science — biology in particular — we understand that every human life begins when a woman's ovum (or egg cell) is fertilised by a man's sperm either through sexual intercourse or by artificial insemination resulting in the formation of an embryo. It is believed that this embryo undergoes a series of transformations in the womb of the woman for an average period of nine months — known as the gestation period — after which it is delivered as a fully developed newborn baby.

While the process described above might indeed be a factual and even accurate representation of the beginning of each human life, what is left unexplained, however, is why a particular sperm cell (out of the 40 million to 1.2 billion released per ejaculation) gets to be the one that eventually fertilises a particular ovum (out of the fifteen to twenty produced by a woman on a monthly basis). We are expected to believe that this occurrence is entirely random and down to chance alone. The truth, however, is that nothing in life is random nor happens by chance.

And so right from the very beginning of life — through human reproduction — we encounter the very first mystery of life: why it was a particular sperm cell that fertilised a particular ovum.

Similarly, although married couples may sometimes regularly engage in sex, it isn't every intercourse that results in a pregnancy. The implication here is that although about a minimum of forty million sperm cells are released per ejaculation and although a likelihood of fifteen or more ova are released singularly at regular intervals during a woman's ovulation period (and therefore available for fertilisation when sexual intercourse occurs during that time), it is still possible that even under such circumstances fertilisation may not occur. How is that ordinarily possible? Considering the very high statistical probability of fertilisation occurring with sexual intercourse during a woman's ovulation period, isn't it rather a mystery that a fertile woman could engage in frequent sexual intercourse month in and month out without getting pregnant? Many married couples have laboured very hard over many years and have patiently awaited a pregnancy all to no avail whereas one night of casual sex, even with just one ejaculation, has resulted in a pregnancy on many different occasions. Another mystery?

Reflecting upon these mysterious realisations, I came to the conclusion that sexual intercourse alone couldn't be responsible for pregnancies or else almost every sexual intercourse would result in a pregnancy. I then realised that sexual intercourse is only a process through which reproduction could be achieved (and possibly the divinely ordained process for that purpose), and I surmised that though a process, it does not on its own have the power to procreate.

And so, we are again faced with another of life's mysteries: Why it is that under similar circumstances, fertilisation only occurs after a particular sexual act and not others. Why did it happen on a given day, date, and time and not on another?

Now, after conception, an embryo begins to form. Medical science — especially biology — have helped to explain the different developmental stages an embryo undergoes while in the womb up to the stage when it is a fully-formed baby ready for delivery. The gestation period takes an average of nine months in humans, meaning that once conception has taken place, nine months later (or thereabouts) the baby should be born.

And while this again might be factual and even accurate, the truth remains that natural birth cannot be accurately predicted with definite certainty — the actual date and time of each baby's arrival cannot be predicted with certainty. Instead, a window of opportunity is suggested based on scientific calculations and assumptions. (Even when a specific date is suggested it is not always the case that the baby arrives on the given date; some babies arrive either earlier or later than the suggested date.) And so it is possible that two babies conceived on the same day and at possibly the same time might be born naturally on different days and times. Why so?

Similarly, while some babies arrive during the estimated ninth month, some other babies arrive before nine months and are referred to as premature babies. Even so, some babies arrive later than nine months, some as late as twelve months or more in some extreme cases. So why are some babies born before the stipulated gestation period of nine months while other babies arrive well after the nine-month period?

Again, reflecting on the foregoing, I could only surmise that just as conception cannot be predicted with certainty, so also can childbirth not be predicted with certainty. Life isn't and can't be governed by scientific calculations and predictions.

The implication of the foregoing facts, is that medical science doesn't have answers to most or all of life's questions rather it would appear that medical science is itself also trying to understand life and, consequently, is in search of answers. It then means that there has to be some other explanation for those aspects of life's many mysteries for which there are no known definite scientific answers, or for which medical science or science in general has no definite answers. There has to be another factor other than the ordinary, natural, or scientific which possibly is responsible for these inexplicable occurrences. And perhaps this other factor is beyond human comprehension, explanation or influence. Perhaps also, it is solely responsible for bringing life into this world.

In my opinion, without any iota of doubt, that factor is what I would like to refer to as "the God factor," and it represents the Almighty, God.

God is the creator of life; just as he is solely responsible for the creation of the first man and woman — whom we know as Adam and Eve — God is also solely responsible for bringing every single human life into the world regardless of the actual process or circumstances through which such a life came into existence. God alone determines who are conceived, by what parents they are conceived, when and where they are conceived, and when and where they are delivered into this world. Every single life would already have been planned by God (who has a particular reason and purpose for creating it) before it would eventually be conceived and delivered.

Incidentally, and to my amazement and satisfaction, I was to also discover that the above opinion had already been expressed in the Holy Bible in the book of Jeremiah 1:5 (KJV):

> Before I formed thee in the belly I knew thee; and before thou camest forth out of the womb I sanctified thee, and I ordained thee a prophet unto the nations.

If I needed any further assurances or confirmation that I was thinking in the right direction, here it was in that single verse of the Bible.

You are not a product of chance.

What do you know about the circumstances of your birth?

Are you a product of the so-called unwanted or unplanned pregnancy, or was your conception lovingly planned and expected? Were you born in wedlock in a stable family unit or outside wedlock in a shaky family structure or to a single parent?

Are you a product of IVF (in vitro fertilisation) or normal fertilisation in the womb? Were you born through natural birth or C- section (caesarean birth)?

Who are your parents? What are their nationalities, ethnicities, origins, backgrounds, social statuses, etc.?

Where were you born? In an impoverished part of the world or in an affluent country? In the so-called developed, developing, or underdeveloped part of the world?

When were you born? The actual day, date and time? The era? The generation?

Whatever your answer is to each of these questions, none of them was a mere random occurrence or a product of ordinary chance. The answers to these questions had all been carefully planned well in advance of your conception and birth, and as difficult as it might be to believe (depending on your unique circumstances), every one of your birth circumstances had been designed and orchestrated specially and specifically for you because of who you were created to be and for the reason you were created.

Let us pause here momentarily for a brief reflection — try reflecting on the peculiar circumstances of your particular birth.

You might ask the following questions: Is it possible that my birth was planned to be the result of an unwanted pregnancy? Was it really planned that I should be born in the generation I was born? So it was planned that I be born a member of a royal family? Are you saying that it was planned that I be born into material poverty and deprivation, into a broken home, or to a single parent?

It may be hard to accept, but in fact the simple truth is that the answer to each of these questions is in the affirmative — as nothing ever happens by chance; instead, the circumstances of your conception and birth were either pre-orchestrated or pre-permitted to happen in the precise way that they eventually did happen. Otherwise it wouldn't have happened in the first place. That, I suppose, is another of life's mysteries.

The natural circumstances of your birth are supposed to help make you who you were created to be. Who you were born as, or even who you are now, isn't necessarily who you are supposed to be — every circumstance we encounter in life is supposed to help transform us into who we are meant to be. And this is because who we are meant to be is the only person who can fulfil the reason for our creation and our purpose. And so instead of bemoaning and lamenting your birth circumstances, embrace them and let them help in transforming you into the person that you should be — which is why you were born under those circumstances in the first place. Denying your birth circumstances is tantamount to denying your existence, and trying to dissociate yourself from them would be like trying to run away from yourself or from your future. Also, envying someone else's birth circumstances and trying to adapt your peculiar circumstances to look like those of the other person's is equivalent to trying to be someone who you are not.

If and when you accept that nothing about you is random, you will acknowledge that everything about you was pre-planned and if so there must then be a reason behind every one of them. Discovering the reasons behind your birth circumstances will help you discover more about yourself and when you discover more of who you are your life will acquire more significance, because it is only then that you would probably begin to understand why this world was graced with your existence you will then discover your purpose.

Everything happens for a reason including our birth circumstances — they each serve a purpose.

Reflect upon the following: Had Nelson Mandela been born in a post-apartheid South Africa would he still have become the person that he became? Or had Barack Obama been born during the seventeenth or eighteenth century would he still have become a president in United States of America? Or had Solomon Northup not been wrongly sold into slavery would he still have been actively involved in the abolitionist movement? Or had Bill Gates been born in Haiti or Ethiopia would he still have founded Microsoft? Would he still have been as rich? Or had Queen Elizabeth II of United Kingdom been born to a different father would she still have been the Queen of England? Or had Rosa Parks been born white would she still have been called "the first lady of civil rights" and "the mother of the freedom movement" by the United States Congress? Would she still have been a well known African-American Civil Rights activist?

These examples are few but they are sufficient to demonstrate that we were born under the peculiar circumstances we were born for a reason; that reason is the very reason we were created and born in the first place.

Chapter 2

Who am I?

Hopefully you probably now understand that you are not a product of an accident or a random occurrence, and that your existence isn't by chance. It is important for you to acknowledge that your birth had been ordained and predestined in advance of its occurrence, and that every of its underlying circumstances has been carefully designed specifically and specially for you.

It is possible that your particular existence might've started from the moment a particular ovum was fertilised by a particular sperm cell but your actual life didn't just start with that fertilisation — every life starts once it has been divinely ordained — and it is this divine ordaining which subsequently makes fertilisation possible. A fact which I suppose has already been demonstrated in the previous chapter — when it was pointed out that it wasn't every sexual intercourse that resulted in a conception — it is even possible that the particular sexual intercourse that resulted in the embryo that eventually became you might've happened in accordance to the divine ordaining that ordained your existence. Similarly, it is also possible that your existence had already been ordained before your parents meet each other or before either of them was even born.

The key issue here is: none of us is here by chance because our existence is the result of a conscious determination and design — of God's plan.

Similarly, the exact day, date, and time you emerged from the womb isn't a product of chance or random occurrence either: it is possible that the timing of your actual birth might've occurred in line with the plan that ordained your existence; it is also possible that your actual birth place is part of that divine plan. I suppose that it will suffice to simply reiterate that nothing about you is random.

Now you may be wondering why your life was preordained, if so be it that it was preordained, and you may wish to ask the following questions: Why me? And, why was I born?

The obvious answer is simply: you were created and born for a reason.

To help demonstrate that you were created for a reason, let me ask you a direct question: Did you play any part in your existence? For instance, did you ask for it? Or were you in any way directly responsible for your existence?

Has it ever occurred to you that you played no part in your existence? That your existence is not a product of your personal choice? None of us desired or asked to be born; none of us decided how, where, when, or by whom we would be born. Instead, those decisions were made for us, not by our parents but by the one who ordained our existence — God. And so it is almost certain that we owe our existence to someone other than ourselves.

If that be the case — that you are in no way responsible for your existence — it is then plausible that you wouldn't possibly know why you were made. Similarly, it is also possible then that you may not know who you truly are since you are not responsible for your constitution and formation. It would require a manufacturer to describe his or her product, including explaining what the product is and what it can be used for, before such a product could be rightly identified, including its rightful use. For instance, a car is unlikely to know what it is or what its functions are, but it would require a car manufacturer's input before someone buying that car would become aware of its various components and also of its numerous capabilities. User's manuals or manufacturer's manuals are usually the medium via which a manufacturer explains his or her products. It means then that since you didn't "construct" yourself you are not likely to know everything there is to know about who you are, including your purpose, except and until you contact your maker — God — requesting such information. Only with the input of your maker would you be able to properly identify yourself.

It is also instructive to note here that before a product is manufactured there would already have been a use or purpose for it and that, as a matter of fact, it is such uses or purposes that would've necessitated the making of that product in the first place. People don't just manufacture things randomly before seeking a use for them. The need — the purpose — often precedes the making; the making (i.e. the what and how), on the other hand, is determined by the need (i.e. the why).

I will like to say that this same principle applies to mankind — you and I — meaning that it is because of our purposes that we are created, and that the who we are is largely determined by the why we are. In other words we are made because of and for our purposes. Consequently, to discover who you are you need the assistance of your creator, God, who alone knows everything about you because it is he who made you.

It is possible that you believe you already know everything you think you need to know about yourself; it is also possible that you believe you know who you are. And so let me ask you another direct question: Who do you think you are?

I suggest you pause for a moment as you try to answer this question.

Having tried answering the above question, would it surprise you if I now suggested to you that the person you think you are is, possibly, not the person you truly are?

And why would I suppose so?

Because we often believe that we are who indeed we are not, and we also often presume to know ourselves very well whereas in truth we might only know very little about ourselves. There are many instances where people who thought they knew themselves very well ended up behaving in ways they didn't expect themselves to behave, or did things that they never believed they were capable of doing when faced with certain situations. For instance, some people who usually described themselves as open-minded might soon discover that they are not really open-minded, when faced with a new ideology. It is often only then that such people might realise that instead of being open-minded they are actually prejudiced or opinionated. Or people who consider themselves to be extroverts might later discover that they prefer spending time alone instead of in the company of others. Similarly, some of those who believed themselves to be selfless might later realise that they mostly are more self-centred than selfless.

So why do we sometimes think that we are who we are not?

I suppose the main reason could be because not many of us actually make the effort to know who we truly are, and so we might simply presume we know ourselves. Another reason could be because most people desire to be those things that are generally accepted as good, positive, and commendable. For instance, those qualities which are generally accepted as virtues are the ones that most people often prefer to identify themselves with; but not many people would want to be described with negative qualities, even where such negative qualities are the ones which they largely exhibit and which would better describe them. Because of this desire of wanting to be identified only with good or positive attributes, most of the time we dwell in our own imaginary fantasies. As a result, even when faced with stark realities as to who we are it often is the case that some people would rather disregard the truth, choosing instead to live in denial while also assuming wrong personalities. And so we might prefer to think that we are open-minded simply because we believe that open-mindedness is more acceptable by popular culture or standards than being opinionated or prejudiced. The same principle might also apply for those other qualities which are popularly regarded as virtues, e.g. selflessness, kindness, friendliness, etc., as it is often the case that some people automatically ascribe these perceived virtues unto themselves whether or not they genuinely posses these qualities.

It is not often that people honestly accept themselves for who they are especially with respect to those qualities that are not considered admirable or positive. Even where such negative qualities might've been acknowledged by the individuals in question it is usually rare that they would publicly admit accordingly, worse still is that they often do nothing about correcting them. Not many people would easily describe themselves as wicked, ill-spirited, murderous, hateful, vengeful, or fraudulent but it is a fact that there are some people whose attitudes generally fit one or more of these descriptions. Or are there not?

Now the danger is that sometimes even when we know who we are, but choose instead to present ourselves as who we are not, it is possible that after a long period of time we might actually begin to believe in our self-deception. Consequently, we may eventually lose sight of our true self while becoming lost in our assumed false identity.

Incidentally, I also found another verse in the Bible which I believe helps to explain the point I am trying to make here, which is Jeremiah 17:9 (KJV):

> The heart is deceitful above all things, and desperately wicked: who can know it?

It would seem that the human mind can be deceitful. And so if you really desire to know your true self, you may have to first overcome this deceitfulness of the human mind by carefully and conscientiously peeling off any masks with which you might've concealed your true identity — masks you might've designed and worn to make you appear better than you really are. We need to unmask ourselves, as it were, if we are to discover the real us because it is only when the mask is off that the real us can be revealed.

Similarly, with respect to our limited knowledge of who we truly are, we need to make conscious efforts to know ourselves: How many times have you taken the time to deliberately have an inward reflection about self? How many times have you tried to consciously understand the type of person that you are? How often do you do a periodic review of your understanding of who you are? It is of vital necessity that we honestly and diligently try to know who we truly are. Without a well-informed knowledge and understanding of who we are it becomes possible and easy to assume any identities simply based on our whims.

A wrong or assumed identity, however, could be dangerous and very risky. It could make us wrongly believe in capabilities and abilities which we do not possess and which might in fact be alien to us. For instance, if a dog believes that it is a lion it risks exposing itself to many avoidable dangers. Imagine such a dog venturing into the jungle acting as if it were a lion. Do you sense any dangers? More so, while it could never truly live the life of a lion, it would also fail to enjoy the life of a dog if it always tried to live as a lion.

Similarly, if a pig believes that it is an eagle and so expects to soar high into the sky you can see that it would've set itself an impossible task. Will believing that it is an eagle make a pig soar up into the skies? I don't think so. That pig would've exposed itself to many avoidable stress and could engage in many exercises in futility all with limited or no productivity.

The following are other but similar scenarios: If a tortoise believes that it is a hare will it run as fast? Will it win a race against a hare? Or if a hen believes that it is a cow who then will lay the eggs? Will that hen produce milk as well? Or if cars are believed to be houses how would we get about? What will become of houses, will they then be driven around?

The main point here is that a wrong identity could be disadvantageous in more ways than one. For instance, it could lead to countless fruitless endeavours, some of which might have required our having to exert ourselves unnecessarily. Similarly, a wrong identity could lead to a wrong application. For instance, if you believe that you are who you are not you are likely to pursue a purpose that is different from the one you are meant for, which in turn could mean that your actual purpose is left unfulfilled.

But remember: it was for that particular purpose you were born.

To better understand who you are, it is important to note that who you are is not limited to your individual personalities alone because many other factors, some of which are external and possibly outside our control, also help to contribute to the composition and constitution of our overall identity. Broadly-speaking, the person that you are is not confined to your natural attributes or qualities but factors such as biological or genetic compositions, origins, nationalities, ethnicities or ancestries, backgrounds, social statuses (of your parents or family), also play significant roles in defining your identity.

Similarly, while the various circumstances of our births might provide the basics of our identities who we are is not necessarily restricted to these circumstances; our true and complete identities evolve as we grow and develop. And so while our identities might be initially founded or based primarily on circumstances beyond our control — our birth circumstances — their overall composition is largely a result of our own determination and contribution, oftentimes as a result of how we handle the various circumstances or situations which we encounter in the process of living life. These contributions — which are within our control — largely determine whether we become who we are meant to be or who we chose to be.

The implication here is that although we are equipped with everything needed to make us who we are meant to be — e.g. birth circumstances and other situations or experiences we subsequently would encounter in life — it is possible to end up differently depending on how we manage those circumstances.

Remember this though: we can only possibly fulfil the purpose of our birth if we become the person who we are meant to be and not otherwise.

It is then instructive to note that perhaps the situations we face in life are all either designed or permitted to befall us so as to assist us become the person we are meant to be. Consequently, how we handle these situations becomes very important as only by handling them positively and productively would they become effective in helping us to become who we are meant to be. Or else handling them wrongly could mean that we become a different person.

The simple truth is that we eventually become the person we choose to become. Another truth is that most of the experiences we encounter in life contribute in making us who we become.

For instance, Nelson Mandela's protracted incarceration in prison could've left him bitter, hateful, or vengeful had he chosen to; fortunately, he chose to allow his imprisonment influence him in other positive ways. Consequently, he became who, as I suppose, he was meant to be and as a result was able to fulfil what I believe to be his purpose (or at least a part of it).

Had Nelson Mandela handled the issue of his twenty-seven years in prison differently, say, instead of allowing that gruesome experience to mellow his previous pro-militant disposition he allowed it to further enrage him leaving him embittered and more militant, he probably would've become a different person to the one whom the world got to know and whom most people respect. Now, imagine what would have become of South Africa with a different Nelson Mandela out of prison: Assuming the Mandela who came out of incarceration was a hateful and vengeful person who was willing to continue the pursuit of his ambition, of a politically-free black South Africa, by any means possible, would apartheid have been brought to an end non-violently or even defeated at all? Would apartheid have been defeated without extreme violence and loss of many lives? Would Nelson Mandela have been able to realise his desire of political freedom for the black people of South Africa? Would Nelson Mandela have become the first black president of the Republic of South Africa? Even so, what type of president would he have been? Finally, what would've become of South Africa with a different Mandela as its president?

Similarly, the biblical Joseph — one of the twelve sons of Jacob — could also have become a different person to the one he became. (Details can be found in Genesis 37 - 47.)

Joseph suffered betrayal in the hands of his hateful and envious brothers, as a result he was sold into slavery and subsequently imprisoned. Joseph could've allowed his various misfortunes to transform him into a bitter, unforgiving, or vengeful individual but instead he chose to look on the brighter side of his dark experiences. Consequently, he was able to accomplish the real and remote objectives of his apparent misfortunes, thereby ultimately fulfilling his purpose in life. Through his ordeal, Egypt, and possibly the rest of the then world, was saved from famine. Through his ordeal also, his entire family subsequently relocated to Egypt where the Hebrew nation would eventually be formed in exile.

None of these would have been possible had Joseph allowed his misfortunes to transform him into someone else. But I suppose he allowed himself to be affected by these rather unfortunate plights the way those plights were expected to affect him because I believe he was allowed to go through those gruesome experiences so that through them he would be transformed into the person he was meant to be, the person who would then be able to accomplish the missions set for him. Simply put, those places and times were not meant to mar but to make him, they were not meant to break but to build him. I believe so also are every circumstances we might encounter in our lives — they are intended to make and build us, not to mar or break us.

Both Nelson Mandela and Joseph found themselves in dire straits and undesirable circumstances, which if handled wrongly could've made them different persons. But, fortunately, they both made the most of very bad situations. It is very important that we also do not despise any circumstances we might find ourselves in, hurriedly wishing them away or allowing them to negatively impact upon us. It is a long-held opinion of mine that there is always something to be benefited from any given situation no matter how bad; even those situations which resulted from our mistakes, recklessness, or carelessness could benefit with us with a lot of positive lessons if handled rightly.

I truly believe everything we encounter in life could help us become the person we are meant to be if handled positively. And so we must endeavour to ensure that we don't allow our misfortunes to turn us into the wrong persons and we must strive to become, through them, the persons we are meant to be.

Looking through history, I observed that most of the people who have gone ahead to accomplish outstanding or exceptional achievements often did so after passing through very difficult circumstances. Most of the world's greats often arrived at greatness through circumstances only a few people would endure. An observation which further confirmed what I have always believed — that the most difficult circumstances often lead to the best outcomes. Treasures are often found in ruins.

I also believe these great men and women probably discovered their real identities in the midst of their various trials.

One more thing I observed while looking through history is that it is often in times of aloneness that greatness is formed in a person. I strongly believe solitude greatly helps us in getting to know who we are because it is often only when we are alone that we are able to have a frank conversation with ourselves. Similarly, it is often when we are alone that we are able to understand ourselves better, and are, eventually, able to figure out who the person inside us is.

The irony, however, is that most of us dread being left alone. Sometimes when we find ourselves alone, we often always seek to engage ourselves in one activity or another if only to keep ourselves and mind preoccupied. It would seem that people often tend to want to distract themselves from themselves — I think it is a common fact that most people dread being alone. Similarly, it is possible the person we mostly dread speaking to is, sadly, our own selves.

Be that as it may, a sincere conversation with self is paramount as it is the most effective way through which you may know who you truly are. This can best be achieved at moments of aloneness or solitude because only then can we really reason with ourselves undisturbed and undistracted. Solitude is not as bad as it sometimes seems. Silence, they say, is golden, I believe so also is solitude.

If you seek to know who you are, I will recommend you make conscious efforts to be alone sometimes. Being alone, amongst its other benefits, helps you to look inwards and to talk with yourself. You really need to start talking with yourself if you desire to know who you are, and frankly too, because talking with yourself is most beneficial when the conversation is an honest one.

As you begin to converse with yourself you might be surprised at how little of yourself you know, you might also realise that most of what you thought you knew about yourself are largely based on assumptions. As your conversation with self progresses you might also realise that there are a few things you cannot unravel on your own; some questions you couldn't answer yourself, and which possibly no one else can help you answer either. We don't have all the answers we need. Similarly, we cannot provide for ourselves all the answers we need. For those questions we need superior assistance, we need divine assistance.

And so as your conversation with self progresses you perhaps will realise the need to involve God. You may even have begun to address God without consciously planning to do so: you may discover yourself asking no one in particular questions you know you have no answers for; at this point, I would imagine your conversation with your maker has already begun. A conversation with God is an absolute necessity if you are to know who you really are. Remember the car and the manufacturer? The car manufacturer knows practically everything about the car; God also knows everything about you because he made you.

Do you know who you are? You could if you tried.

Chapter 3

Why am I here?

In the last chapter it was demonstrated that we are not responsible for our existence — no individual orchestrated his or her birth. We are simply born, we just happen to find ourselves here.

Consequently, it would be difficult, almost impossible, to accurately state, independently, why you are here. You may hazard guesses, make some reasonable assumptions, or speculate variously but you cannot be absolutely certain. At least, not if such endeavours are void of divine participation. But it is possible to discover exactly why you are here.

So, why are you here? What are you doing here?

The obvious answer to the first question is reasonably simple and straightforward: You are here because God brought you here. The answer to the second question, however, is not as simple or straightforward. Following the answer to the first question, however, it is possible to arrive at a correct answer to the latter question.

God brought you here, and he must've done so for a reason.

Recall that in the last chapter it was demonstrated that need or purpose preceded manufacturing or creation. It was argued that before a thing is made there would've been a need for it. And so I am inclined to believe that we are created, mainly, as a result of the need we are born to satisfy or fulfil. Put in another way, our creation is occasioned by our purpose. It is very unlikely that we are first born before a purpose is then decided for us, but it is more reasonable to believe that we are born because there was a need which necessitated our creation.

With that in mind, it follows that for us to discover why we are here we have to carefully acquaint ourselves with the circumstances of our birth and simply because, if we are born to fulfil a purpose we are more likely to be born under the circumstances — times, places, backgrounds, experiences, privileges, opportunities, etc. — which would facilitate or enhance the fulfilment of such purposes. For instance, a ship is more likely to be constructed in an area with a sea nearby, not in a desert. Also, houses are more likely to be built in places suitable for human habitation (e.g. mainland areas), not offshore or peaks (e.g. mountain tops or polar extremes). Similarly, rainproof clothing and umbrellas are more likely to be traded in areas with regular seasonal rainfalls than in arid regions. Also, heaters are more likely to be installed in houses built in temperate regions while flood barriers and storm breakers are more likely to be put in place in coastal areas. Plants which depend on a lot of water for their development are often grown in rainforests while those which thrive on limited supply of water are often planted in arid regions.

These few examples help to demonstrate the close relationship that exists between purpose and identity. It is possible that by knowing what something is it would become easier to also know what it is used for. Similarly, other factors (e.g. location, seasonal occurrence, structure, composition, design, strength, size, etc.) could help in discovering the use for a thing.

I believe this same principle applies to us, as humans, as our purposes and identities are intricately related: We are who we are because of why we are; we are where we are because of why we are; we experience the things we do because of why we are; we are privileged with the things we are privileged with because of why we are; we are how we are because of why we are. Possibly everything about us is because of why we are.

And so I believe that in getting to know who we truly are we would also discover why we are born. I would imagine that everything that makes us who we are — including our birth circumstances and our individual experiences — hold the secret of why we are.

To help demonstrate this dependence between identity and purpose, I will refer to the story of Moses in the Bible. (Details can be found in Exodus 2 – 14.)

Moses was born of Hebrew parents — and therefore a Hebrew — in Egypt. His birth came at a time a decree (to kill every male born Hebrew child) was in place. However, instead of surrendering the newborn baby to the Egyptian authorities, as required by law, his mother decided to hide Moses because she saw that he was a fine or good-looking child.

Moses was hid by the bank of River Nile. Subsequently, he was discovered by Pharaoh's daughter who decided to adopt him even though she suspected that he was a Hebrew child (Exodus 2:6). Incidentally, it was Moses' biological mother that Pharaoh's daughter would subsequently entrust with his nursing and upbringing. And so although born a Hebrew, Moses would effectively become an Egyptian prince, and placed in the line of succession.

However, as the story progresses, it would be observed that Moses' primary purpose was possibly to lead the nascent Hebrew nation formed in captivity in Egypt out of captivity into its promised land, which I suppose was a significant reason for the birth of Moses.

(Reflecting upon the life of Moses, it struck me how what I believe to be his purpose was delicately hinged upon his true identity: Moses' true identity is Hebrew even though he was an Egyptian prince growing up. I wondered if Moses had been made to believe that he was truly the son of Pharaoh's daughter (and therefore an Egyptian by ancestry) whether the story would have ended differently. Assuming a wrong identity would probably have meant that Moses wouldn't have done the things he subsequently did especially the thing he did which necessitated his fleeing into exile.)

Moses got involved in a fight between an Egyptian and a Hebrew where he joined forces with the Hebrew killing the Egyptian. I believe Moses action here was inspired by his awareness of his true identity because had he believed himself to be Egyptian, he probably would've sided with the Egyptian instead. In another incident which involved a fight between two Hebrews, Moses would admonish the two fighters chiding them for fighting with each other, seeing that they were both Hebrews, and as a result was rebuffed by the guilty of the two fighters who wanted to know if he (Moses) had intended to kill him as he had killed the Egyptian previously. When Moses discovered that his earlier conspiracy wasn't the secret he presumed it was he fled Egypt.

Moses left the comfort of Pharaoh's palace for a life of uncertainty in the wilderness. It must've been a dire strait for him as well as a big shock since he now had to scrounge for his existence whereas he had lived in abundance at the palace. Incidentally, it was in the wilderness that Moses would first become acquainted with his purpose — at the right time Moses had an encounter with God while at the wilderness, during which he was expressly intimated with his mission to liberate the Hebrews from slavery in Egypt. I also personally believe that it was in the wilderness that Moses also got to discover more about who he was.

And so Moses' purpose was intricately linked with his true identity such that for him to be able to properly identify his purpose he needed to first know who he truly was, and not who he might've presumed that he was or who he might've been at a time (e.g. an Egyptian prince).

(And so in addition to helping to demonstrate the relationship between purpose and identity, the story of Moses also lends weight to the belief that solitude and very difficult situations both play significant roles in shaping our identities and by extension our destinies even when such situations result from our mistakes, as in the case of Moses here.)

Back to the story…

After God instructed Moses with what he was required to do, after an initial reluctance, he went back to Egypt, this time to request Pharaoh to release the Hebrews under his captivity. Although he initially came face to face with a stiff opposition from Pharaoh, he was eventually able to fulfil his mission — he led the young Hebrew nation out of captivity into independence. End of story.

I suppose there are many lessons to be learnt from this story but a very significant one (which is more relevant to our current discussion) is that for Moses to identify and fulfil his purpose he first needed to know who he truly was. For Moses to know why he was — in this case, to led the Hebrew nation out of captivity — he had to know who he was — a Hebrew, not an Egyptian prince.

This clearly demonstrates how why we are is closely related and connected with who we are.

On the other hand, note how the various experiences Moses would subsequently encounter following his birth also greatly contributed in shaping him into becoming the right person to fulfil the mission assigned to him.

As highlighted in the last chapter, in addition to our particular birth circumstances most of the other things we would subsequently encounter in life play significant roles in shaping our overall identity — we become who we are not only as a result of our birth circumstances but also as a result of how we handle the other circumstances we might encounter as our lives progress. It was also pointed out that most of those other circumstances would equip us for the performance of our purposes if properly handled, meaning that it is somehow possible to understand our purposes — why we are here — by carefully taking into account our non-birth circumstances.

In the case of Moses, who wasn't born a royalty, his adoption by Pharaoh's daughter gave him the privilege of royalty. Consequently, he had the opportunity for trainings in leadership — a vital requirement for the role he would eventually play. Similarly, Moses' exile in the wilderness provided him with opportunities for other forms of cognitive trainings required for his overall purpose. For instance, in the wilderness Moses became a shepherd who looked after his father-in-law's flocks. To be a good shepherd a person has to learn to be patient, caring, gentle, tolerant, and more — qualities, all of which would be needed in the performance of his duties as a national leader. Finally, Moses' wilderness experience exposed him to suffering, the type of suffering he could never have experienced in Pharaoh's palace. I suppose his time in the wilderness would've exposed him to hunger, lack, deprivation, fear, anxiety, etc., thereby helping him to become more humane and empathetic. It may also have helped in humbling him, helping to transform him into the meek person that he would later become (Numbers 12:3) — all vital requirements for a leader of people.

And so we see how the circumstances Moses would encounter later in life provided him with prerequisite experience necessary for the performance and fulfilment of his purpose. It would seem as though his various experiences (including his birth circumstances) were pointers to why Moses was born — or, why he was here.

It then means that in order to discover why you are here, you have to thoroughly explore the makings of who you are including your birth and other circumstances.

Before putting aside the story of Moses, let me also use it to illustrate an opinion I expressed earlier — the one about nothing in life (including the circumstances of our birth) being random and that there is a reason for everything we eventually experience in life.

Please try reflecting upon the following:

- Moses was supposed to have been killed soon after he was born, in accordance with a prevailing decree at the time, but he wasn't because his mother decided to hide him. Why?
- Moses' mother took a great risk in violating one of the laws of the land in which she was a refugee. She was willing to risk her life to preserve Moses. Why?

- Moses was put in a basket and laid on the bank of the Nile river. Had he been discovered by a wrong person it would've been over for his young life, and probably over for his mother as well and maybe even for his entire family. But, fortunately, he wasn't discovered by a wrong person. Similarly, he could've been swept away by a rogue current or attacked by a crocodile or fish but, again, none of these happened. Why?
- It was Pharaoh's daughter who discovered Moses and she instantly took a liking to him and decided to keep him. Why?
- The responsibility for Moses' upbringing fell upon his biological mother, of all other possibilities. Why?
- Moses grew up in Pharaoh's palace as a prince thereby becoming trained in leadership and management. Why?
- He later fled the palace and Egypt into the wilderness where he became a shepherd, a vocation which further equipped him with more and different leadership skills. Why?

Is it possible any of these occurrences was random? Think again.

I suppose this at least helps to show that everything happens for a reason and nothing happens by chance or a random coincidence.

As it was with Moses, so it is with all of us: nothing has ever happened to us by chance, nothing also has ever happened to us without a reason. If you would care to reflect upon your own life you probably would realise nothing about you is random. You probably would also realise there was a reason behind everything that has happened to you. Similarly, everything that will happen to you now, and later all have their respective reasons.

It is possible to know why you are here.

Once you discover your true identity you would've also discovered a greater part of your purpose if not its entirety.

Let me now make this vital clarification: you are not here for just a single reason. An individual's purpose is not singular. A person's purpose — why we are here — is made up of multiple individual or specific purposes, some of which sometimes are independent of the other purposes and some of which at other times are interconnected and interrelated.

Sometimes one or more components of our overall purpose may be so monumental they could risk overshadowing the other relatively smaller components. In such cases it is possible to wrongly assume that such mega components are our only purpose. The truth, however, is that our overall purpose is more than just a single mission; it is a complex web of numerous missions, some big others relatively small.

In such cases also, it is possible to wrongly assume that the mega components of our overall purpose is more important than other relatively minor components. It is my opinion, however, that every aspect of our individual purposes are of equal importance even though some might appear greater than others, because in reality none is superior to the other or more important than another.

I also believe that we begin to fulfil our purposes the moment we are born, even if unbeknownst to us that we may be doing so.

To help illustrate the foregoing points, I will refer to the story of Joseph whom I already cited earlier:

Joseph became instrumental in bringing the rest of his family down to Egypt to escape a famine, a move that was necessary for the eventual formation of the Hebrew nation.

However, additionally, Joseph was also instrumental in preserving Egypt (and possibly the rest of the then world also) from famine.

These two instances represent different components of Joseph's overall purpose. Both could rightly be regarded as monumental because they are indeed each great responsibilities. But they couldn't truly diminish other components of his overall purpose which are equally important in their own rights, even if not as apparently great as these two.

For instance, Joseph was also father to Ephraim and Manasseh both of whom, I suppose, also have their respective purposes in life. By contributing to their birth Joseph somehow also fulfils another purpose.

Similarly, Joseph was husband to Asenath — a Pharaoh's daughter — and being a husband to her possibly is yet another purpose.

Also Joseph helped the chief butler interpret his dreams, brought about some positive changes and progress in the house of Potiphar, whom he one-time served, during the period of his service there, must've positively influenced other inmates whom he would've met in the prison while in prison, and would've also positively affected his brothers who sold him into slavery by his gracious act of forgiveness towards them.

And the list could go on.

These few examples, however, should suffice in showing the complex nature of the overall purpose of each individual, and in revealing that although some of them might appear greater than some others all of them are nonetheless equally important.

A very significant implication here is that in trying to discover why we are here, we have to first realise that we are not here for just a single reason. We are here for a whole lot of reasons which all make up our overall purpose, some of which might be interconnected and others which might seem to be standalones but all of which are of equal importance.

It is my opinion that there is something for us to do each day we are alive. I also believe that if we can sincerely and diligently do anything and everything that is within our powers to do, each time, all the time, to the best of our abilities we probably would already be satisfying or fulfilling the many reasons why we are here. An opinion which seems to have been echoed by King Solomon in Ecclesiastes 9:10 (KJV):

> Whatsoever thy hand findeth to do, do it with thy might; for there is no work, nor device, nor knowledge, nor wisdom, in the grave, whither thou goest.

I also believe that we are not here to satisfy ourselves alone but that we are also here to satisfy one another for the overall benefit of humanity. Consequently, in doing all we do it is very important not to do them for selfish reasons or with ulterior motives, but for the simple reason that they are the right things to do. We should do good for goodness sake alone. We shouldn't really be concerned with who gets credit for our actions or whether or not we are appreciated or our deeds acknowledged.

I believe that if we faithfully do whatever we can, when we can, how best we can, for the sake of doing the right thing and not with ulterior motives then our little deeds would eventually lead us to greater achievements.

Which, incidentally, was exactly what happened in the case of Joseph:

Joseph was sold into slavery by his brothers, nevertheless, in spite of his misfortune, he remained diligent which subsequently led to his promotion in his master's house. He later became wrongfully imprisoned but his unjust treatment didn't deter or diminish his diligence. In prison he continued to be diligent, which again led to his promotion. He interpreted Pharaoh's butler's dreams while in prison and as a result he was recommended to Pharaoh, this led to his release from prison and promotion to a ministerial position in Egypt.

Could Joseph have expected that his diligence would eventually yield such dividends? But they did and in a manner he could never have imagined.

Why are you here?

I would imagine you are here to do every good that you can, whenever you can, how best you can, and not for selfish reasons but for the sake of goodness alone and for the benefit of humanity in general. And as you diligently perform each responsibility, no matter how small or insignificant, accomplishing each mission it will lead you to other responsibilities and missions. Step by step, slow but steady, little by little you will move from missions to missions until you perform your very last mission after which you probably would've fulfilled your overall purpose. This might sound very simplistic but the truth, however, is that in reality it is not entirely as complicated as it sometimes seems.

That, I suppose, is the general overview but the actual details would be up to you to discover as it is only you who could discover these daily responsibilities or missions, as they apply to you, and having discovered them to diligently perform them.

Part Two

The Journey

Thy word is a lamp unto my feet, and a light unto my path.

Psalm 119:105 (KJV)

Chapter 4

Where from? Where to?

Life oftentimes has been described as a journey; from all indications this seems to be the case, because not a single person has continued to remain in the world since its very beginning. Instead, people come and people go and in that sense life indeed seems to be a journey.

With journeys, however, there is usually a beginning, the process or actual travelling, and an end. Journeys don't usually last forever. Similarly, life — as a journey — also has a beginning, a process, and an end. Life it can be said begins at birth, then progresses before eventually terminating at death.

That much is pretty obvious. What might not be similarly obvious, however, is the answer to the question: where do we come from?

Where are you from? And where are you going? Wouldn't you like to know?

But is it really necessary to know where you are from and where you are going? Couldn't we simply continue with our lives without bothering ourselves with those questions? I guess we could. It may not be important after all knowing where we are from or where we are going.

But would it really be prudent living without knowing where we are from or where we are going?

If life indeed is a journey, it wouldn't be wise ignoring both questions because the knowledge of the starting point as well as the destination is very significant and relevant for the successful completion of any journey. Without these two vital information — the starting point and destination — planning a journey would almost be impossible. Failing to plan for a journey, or making insufficient or ineffective plans, in turn, would most likely result in a difficult and complicated journey at best, but could actually result in an unsuccessful journey. Oftentimes, before we commence on a journey the first thing we usually do is to first determine our destination — where do I want to go? — and having first established a destination it becomes easier planning how to get there. To decide how best or fast to get to our destination we normally would have to determine where we currently are — where am I? — and to help us determine where we currently are (in cases where we are not sure about our current location), knowing where we are coming from is often very helpful.

I suppose this is why oftentimes when we make enquiries about directions for a particular journey, the following information are often required from us: The first usually is our destination — where are you going? — and the second is almost always our location — where are you? And if peradventure we are unable to identify our current location (maybe because we are somehow lost in transit), the information that is often required would be where we started our journey — where are you coming from? The knowledge of where a person started his or her journey is very useful in helping to determine his or her current location, because it is possible that by retracing his or her steps his or her current location could be rightly identified.

It is often said that to know where you're going you need to first know where you are; to know where you are you need to first know where you're coming from. And so it seems reasonable to conclude that to know where you're going you need to first know where you're coming from.

We shall therefore start with the first of the two questions — where are you from?

Where from?

The simple truth is that no one can say with absolute certainty that he or she knows where exactly he or she is from. And this might be so because before our conception and subsequent birth we didn't really exist — at least not in a physical form. However, the origin of mankind is accounted for in the Bible:

> And God said, Let us make man in our image, after our likeness: and let them have dominion over the fish of the sea, and over the fowl of the air, and over the cattle, and over all the earth, and over every creeping thing that creepeth upon the earth.
> So God created man in his own image, in the image of God created he him; male and female created he them.
> Genesis 1:26, 27 (KJV).

From the above piece of information it can be deduced that man is a product of God's design. We are the product of an idea in the mind of God. Consequently, it can be said that we are from God — from God's plan. A fact further confirmed in Jeremiah 1:5 (KJV):

> Before I formed thee in the belly I knew thee; and before thou camest forth out of the womb I sanctified thee, and I ordained thee a prophet unto the nations.

We are from the mind of God — an idea or a plan of God's.

That is the basic truth, as simple as it might seem. Consequently, the entirety of our existence revolves around this vital truth — that we are all products of divine design and plan — and our success in life depends largely on whether or not we live in accordance with the divine plan that occasioned our lives.

Remember: A product's usefulness can only be maximised when that product is applied strictly in accordance with the purpose it was made for.

Although a product could still be put to other uses, it can only yield the best results when used for its rightful purpose. I believe the same principle applies to humans, meaning that we can only get the best out of our lives when we live in accordance with the divine plan and design that brought us into existence. Anything else, in my opinion, would lead to a mediocre existence and an unfulfilled life regardless of our material successes.

Now let us tackle the second question — where are you going?

The destination of a journey gives meaning to the journey itself and it makes the journey more worthwhile. Similarly, a journey without a known destination is likely to be a daunting prospect but setting and knowing a destination makes a journey possible, easier, pleasurable, as well as meaningful.

A destination, and the knowledge of it, can also be a strong motivational factor during the journey: knowing where you are going would help to dissuade you from aborting your journey midway if for instance, you encounter difficulties along the way. You are more likely to successfully complete a journey, against all odds, when you know your destination and when you are determined to get to that destination. Otherwise, it is easier to simply abort a journey midway when faced with obstacles when there is no known or definite destination. For instance, with a known destination you are not likely to terminate a journey simply because, say, you encountered a storm or a network of bad roads along your way. The knowledge that you are yet to arrive at your objective would help to keep you moving on, especially when you are determined to get to your destination. As a matter of fact, it often is the case that the knowledge that such obstacles must be overcome if you have to get to your destination actually helps to motivate you to overcome them.

Similarly, knowing your destination would help to ensure that you don't end up at the wrong place or just anywhere.

And so it would seem that knowing where we are going is as important as knowing where we are from.

Where to?

Again, no one can truly say with absolute certainty that he or she knows exactly where people go to once they depart from this world. However, having established where we are from — the mind of God — the knowledge of where we are going somehow becomes obvious and certain. If we came from God then it is only sensible and reasonable to expect that we would be returning to God — we are going back to where we came from, God. A sentiment echoed in Ecclesiastes 12:7 (KJV):

> Then shall the dust return to the earth as it was: and the spirit shall return unto God who gave it.

It is that simple.

Having now established our coordinates, as it were, in that we have now identified our starting point — where from? — and our destination — where to? — the actual journey itself should now be relatively easier, filled with more prospects, more meaningful, and also more satisfying.

Let us now commence the actual journey. Adventures await.

Chapter 5

Rat race

We sometimes refer to living in the world as a "rat race" where people jostle and struggle in pursuit of a better life, often engaged in an imaginary competition with one another and this comparison of life with a race (rat race) may seem appropriate especially taking into consideration the fact that most of us live as though life is a fierce competition where almost every other person is a rival. Sometimes it does seem as though the only way to succeed in life is by outdoing our contemporaries or that success is defined by having more material possessions than our contemporaries.

And so in that sense: life seems indeed to be a race.

But is life truly a race, let alone a rat race? Is it possible that life was designed by the creator — God — to be a race? You may wish to reflect on this rhetoric question for a moment.

Whether or not God intended life to be a race, the reality, as sad as it may be, is that we seem to have made a rat race of our lives:

Almost as soon as a child is born, they are inadvertently initiated into a life of struggle. Ironically, most people arrive this world through a different type of struggle — the labour that often takes place before childbirth — and as if in acknowledgement of that struggle, the first sound almost every child makes upon arriving the world is a very loud shrill cry. (Could it be there is more to this than we already know? Could our very first sound — a cry — hold deeper significance? Could it be a sign of things to come? Could it be a child's way of protesting that the world it is born into is not the one originally intended?)

It may well be that a child arrives the world crying for very good reasons because a closer look at the world and life we have imposed upon ourselves and our children leaves much to be desired and deserves a few tears. Maybe even some wails as most children do upon being born.

Many children — especially those born in recent generations — do not enjoy the type of lifestyle that supposedly makes for an ideal childhood. Many are denied the right amount of parental bonding (especially maternal bonding) as a result of the limited amount of time most parents are opportune to spend with their children. Work, career, and other secular activities tend to deny some parents sufficient time with their children starting from very early stages.

Children depend greatly on nurturing, caring, loving and close associations and interactions most of which are naturally provided by parents — for their growth and development. Children learn mostly by observation — they watch, learn, and emulate — which means an intimate and, more importantly, personal relationship with their parents is an important natural necessity for a proper growth and development of children. A child needs a direct and one-on-one interaction with an adult — especially their parents — for its overall growth and development. A group or general approach to nurturing children is often ineffective in ensuring their proper development as oftentimes this approach fails to provide the right level of personal interactions needed to help each child properly understand the many things about life it needs to know as it grows.

Permit me to suggest that nurturing children and ensuring their proper overall development is a parental responsibility — a divinely-established natural responsibility.

Unfortunately, however, occasioned by our being caught up in the so-called rat race, most children are often denied the benefit of this parental responsibility which I believe is the right and entitlement of every child. Some children often face neglect where they require more attention, others lack the comfort and protection provided by constant bodily contact with their parents, while some are simply left to their own devices as they explore new environments, in which they often find themselves, unaided and unguided. All of which exert a huge toll on the overall development of the affected children.

Children brought up under such circumstances — lack of adequate parental presence in their upbringing — often struggle in the later stages of their lives as they are forced to learn by experiences earned (by themselves and often at great personal costs) rather than gained (from their parents during and through their upbringing).

Similarly, some children are committed to the care of professional child carers or minders while their parents get more involved in the rat race. While the services provided by many professionals in childcare are commendable, in that they help to bridge an important gap, they cannot, however, serve as a perfect substitute for parental care nor are they equally as effective as parental care. For instance, such services do not facilitate parent-child bonding which greatly assists with a child's emotional and psychological growth, development and wellbeing.

Another unfavourable consequence of professional childcare — especially those operating commercially — is that it launches the affected children starting from a very early age into a lifestyle and regime best suited for adults. It often is the case that such children are taken to their minders very early each weekday as their parents travel to their respective workplaces or businesses. As a result such children are often woken up very early in the mornings (at times that they should still be enjoying their sleep) and are hurriedly prepared for a day at the crèche, nursery, or childminder's; their feeding might also be affected (e.g. the content, quantity, and timing) and they are generally exposed to environments and conditions that are not ideal for children their age.

The overall implication is that children exposed very early to professional childcare are often denied the right degree of freedom that most children are entitled to and instead are exposed to one limitation (or restriction) or another. For instance, they may not be free to explore their immediate environments as much as they probably would've wanted to. Or their crèche environments may be limited in space or may be lacking in various facilities that are easily available in many homes and with which children engage their many curiosities as they seek to know more about the world they have found themselves in. Even at their bests, crèches or nurseries couldn't still compare with homes and the environment at homes. These limiting conditions and more could significantly affect a child's overall growth and development.

The overall impact of a lack of more direct involvement of parents in the nurturing and upbringing of their children — especially during early childhood when children need more intimate and personal care — is that most children are left ill-equipped to face life, mainly because of improper and inadequate mental or psychological and other growth and development.

Additionally, another negative consequence here is that many children are inadvertently inculcated with wrong ideologies — learnt from how their parents conduct their lives — and especially that of life as a rat race. Children often start very early to believe in the idea that life is a rat race simply by observing their parents live life as a rat race.

And so in addition to poor mental and other development, most people are also exposed to wrong sets of ideologies very early in life which they imbibe, meaning that such people start life very wrongly and inadequately equipped mentally and otherwise.

With that not-so-solid foundation and shaky beginning we are launched into life where we would encounter even more damaging ideologies. By regarding life as a race, it is wrongly perceived as a competition with the implication that most people grow up with the wrong belief that in order to be successful in life they have to excel over their contemporaries. Such people wrongly believe that for them to have a good life they must triumph over others and that outdoing their contemporaries by acquiring more material possessions than them equates to a successful living. Consequently, almost every other person is seen as a rival — the opponents that have to be defeated in the race — while their overriding ambition, motivation, and inspiration is to do better than others — to win.

Ironically, this spirit of competition seems to be further encouraged by the first societal system or institution children are initially exposed to as they are introduced to a wider world — the educational system:

Our educational system tends to encourage rivalry (howbeit a healthy type, as I would imagine) as its modes of assessment seem to pitch those involved against one another. Starting from nursery education and through to universities and other higher institutions we are exposed to one form of competition or another. Our academic performances are weighed against the performances of our contemporaries and those who perform exceptionally or outstandingly are recognised in many different ways (e.g. prizes, promotions, awards, scholarships, etc.), while the underperformers are encouraged to emulate the high achievers. Our performances in extracurricular activities are similarly compared with the performances of our contemporaries. For instance, in order to qualify for selection as part of an athletic team one has to do better than the others equally seeking to be selected. Similarly, it is often the quickest runners who are chosen to represent either a school or particular groups in a school (e.g. faculties, departments, boarding houses, etc.) in race competitions.

Our educational system seems to be all about doing better than our contemporaries — winning or excelling — which seems to further enshrine life in our young minds as a competition.

And so our very first exposure to the bigger world — outside the family structure — as we continue in the journey of life as young people tends to confirm to us what we have already wrongly assumed from home about life — that it is a race and therefore a competition. Consequently, we grow up believing life is all about doing better than others. Which, unfortunately, seems to be the mindset with which we begin life and which eventually would become our most underlying and overriding attitude or mindset as we journey through life.

The family system and the educational system provide the main basis for a child's overall development. These institutions are a child's primary contact in a world that is alien to it and they both largely determine how as children we view that world. It is from the family system and the educational system that most children learn almost everything they get to learn in the early stages of their lives. We are largely products of whatever brands of both systems that we are a part of.

These two systems play very significant roles in shaping our minds and they greatly influence our general perception of life. Children whose parents live as though life is a rat race and who subsequently passed through an educational system which tends to encourage competition would most likely grow up with the wrong mentality which supposes life as a competition. Consequently, such children would uphold this wrong ideology as they progress in life and might continue to do so till the end except they are corrected somehow and sometime.

It is instructive to note that I am not blaming our family and educational systems here (even though both could do with one or more improvements here and there), my main consideration, instead, is to demonstrate how we might've been affected by these systems.

And so, the key thing here is: for us to check ourselves in order to determine the extent to which we might've been influenced by both the type of upbringing we have had at home and the type of education we have received. We need to truly ascertain how much of this damaging mindset — competitive mindset — we might've wrongly imbibed as a result of our early childhood, upbringing and growing up. It is a vital necessity that you correctly ascertain where you stand with respect to this mindset because if left uncorrected it could greatly undermine the overall quality of your life. But before it could be corrected or rectified it must first be properly identified — hence the need to know if and by how much you might've been affected with this mindset.

It is possible you have always viewed life as a competition and it is also possible that you believe the only way to succeed in life is by outperforming your contemporaries. You may see life as a rat race, you may also be striving very hard to win that race.

And if you are, don't be surprised because you are not alone since it is possible there are many more people who also uphold a similar mentality. Also don't be too hard on yourself because it wasn't probably your fault you are inculcated with this wrong ideology — you may simply have become a victim of your circumstances.

What must be done, however, is a turnaround, and for this you are solely responsible. The most effective remedy for a wrong mindset is to change it. To change it, however, you must first identity and acknowledge it; then you must also be willing to change it and such willingness must be backed up with action — taking the necessary steps required to effect a positive change. All of which only you can do for yourself. It means that, although you might've become a victim not by choice, you can only remain a victim if you choose so.

The rat race mentality is as unhealthy — it is divisive, counterproductive, limiting, and exerting — as it is wrong. Sadly, it seems to be common and very popular.

With a mindset that views life as a rat race you are likely to struggle more than necessary, as you will constantly and continuously strive to outdo others. Similarly, regarding almost every other person as a rival would mean that you may deny yourself the many benefits that could accrue to partnerships and cooperatives. Many times we achieve more by combining our efforts with those of others than is possible when we rely on solitary efforts alone.

Furthermore, failing to rectify the rat race mentality — where it exists — could mean that it is unwittingly passed on to our children or other minors under our sphere of influence, with the implication that this negative mindset could then be perpetuated down many generations.

I believe the world would be a better place if no one sees life as a rat race. Life is not a race, definitely not a rat race.

If life was meant to be a race then many things wouldn't be the way they now are. For instance, we would all have been born the same or very similar — with equal abilities, capabilities, opportunities, experiences, circumstances, etc. — and we would've been provided with the set of rules, regulations, and guidelines governing the competition. More so, we would've been told what the winning prize is. And to motivate us, we would've been given names of past winners. These would at least help to ensure the competition is fair. It wouldn't be fair pitching a tortoise against a hare in a race competition, would it? It wouldn't be fair matching a lion against a lamb in a fight, would it?

These, however, do not seem to be the case as we are all unique individuals with different sets of abilities, capabilities, opportunities, experiences, and circumstances.

I believe one of the reasons we are made different from each other is so that we would complement each other (by cooperating together) and not to compete against each other. We are gifted with different abilities and skills to encourage partnership, not rivalry.

We need to put aside the rat race mentality and maybe then we would experience an entirely different life.

Life is not a rat race, it is not a competition.

Chapter 6

Mind control

The human mind is powerful, very powerful: through the mind a person can easily be influenced or controlled; through the mind also, a multitude of people can easily be controlled; through the mind an entire generation or many generations could be brought under one influence or another. It is possible to exercise control through influencing the mind because the mind controls actions.

Every thing we do is first processed in the mind before the actual action is implemented — thought precedes action. It is not likely actions can independently be executed without first conceiving them in the mind. Sometimes the processing which takes place in the mind occurs subconsciously or spontaneously so that it is possible we are unaware it is happening. Most times, however, the processing that goes on in our minds are not only conscious but are also durable.

Thoughts are processed in the mind, a process referred to as thinking, and the ability to think is generally considered a higher level of intelligence. Being able to think independently, however, is what qualifies a person as an individual — a distinct or separate entity. If our thinking is brought under or exposed to any undue influences which inhibit our capability of being able to think independently — original and self-inspired — such that our thinking is remotely controlled or guided externally, in such a state we can no longer rightly be described as individuals. For instance, if such external influences guide or manipulate our thinking in a particular pattern or towards an expected outcome, under such circumstances we would better be described as part of a group and not as individuals.

I could say the fundamental criterion which distinguishes an individual from a group of people is the ability to think independently. Hence the renowned French philosopher, Rene Descartes, stated in Latin:

"Cogito, ergo sum." (Discourse on Method;1637)

Which simply translates to English as:

"I think, therefore I am."

The significance of an independent mind could never be overemphasised: In the absence of an independent mind — one free of any forms of control — we risk being reduced to mere puppets easily controllable by whatever or whoever controls our minds. I could say, very much like zombies who simply emulate the actions of other zombies without knowing why those other zombies are doing what they are doing.

I suppose there is a very good reason why each of us is equipped with a mind — we all have our own minds. In my opinion, the reason is to enable us take full and sole responsibility of and for our actions. With a mind that belongs to you it would be difficult blaming someone else for your own actions, especially since actions derive from thoughts which in turn are processed in the mind. And so if you have your own mind you couldn't possibly deny responsibility for how it is used.

Living comprises of series of actions, actions are products of thoughts, thoughts are processed in the human mind. Therefore, it could be argued that life is essentially in the mind.

It means that the right and proper development of the mind is key to living a good life. Consequently, great care ought to be taken in ensuring that our minds properly grow and develop starting from the moment we are born.

I suppose a significant part of the proper development of the mind would be in ensuring that the independence of each child's mind is well protected as he or she grows. In other words, children ought to be encouraged to use their minds independently, howbeit ably and appropriately assisted by responsible older and wiser adults.

It would seem, however, that this is not usually the case in practice. It is a common experience that as children we are often subjected to a high level of control. While this level of control is largely aimed for our protection — since children often cannot appreciate dangerous circumstances — it nonetheless has its disadvantages especially when exercised in excess.

Almost as soon as we are born we are brought under the control of our parents — as they try to think for us: what and when to eat, what to wear, when to play, who to play with, sleeping arrangements, etc. — who try to do everything possible to ensure our maximum comfort and protection. Sometimes when we even try to protest a particular thing or to communicate something, say, by crying we are often cajoled by our parents to stop us from crying while they try to figure out for themselves what we might've been trying to relate to them. It is understandable that these actions of our parents are often done in good faith, with positive intentions, and for our benefit but at the same time they affect us, as children, in other ways not all of which are positive.

Please note that I am not condemning the controlling nature of some parental responsibilities and duty of care, my sole intention, instead, is to simply point out how such common, sincere, and innocent behaviours could negatively impact on the proper development of a child's mind especially with respect to ensuring the independence of the mind.

By doing almost everything for us as children — including trying to think for us — it is possible that the independent use of our young minds is slightly inhibited as we learn to rely on our parents and their thoughts and opinions. Ultimately, we learn to do as told without asking why and we learn to wholly accept the opinions of our parents. This practice of a wholesome acceptance of the ideas and opinions of our parents gradually denies us the independent use of our own minds. And failing to think independently for ourselves could eventually render us somewhat conditioned — we might get used to being thought for, thereby failing to try thinking for ourselves at other times and possibly in the future greatly impacting negatively on an independent use of our minds. We may simply fail to realise how to apply our minds independently or we may simply neglect doing so out of habit.

While it might be appropriate for parents to think for their children during early childhood, especially when such children are too young to distinguish between right and wrong, the real issue, however, is knowing how best to and also when best to stop thinking for a child. It is important that while assisting very young children make decisions they are also encouraged to participate in the decision-making process, no matter how minimal a contribution they are able to make, so that very early in life they are able to engage their own minds in processing thoughts. It is important that from a very early stage children are encouraged to use their minds to think independently.

Remember: I think, therefore I am.

For a child to be — exist as an individual — he or she has to learn to think — independently. Consequently, due diligence ought to be taken by parents, as they do their best in bringing up their children, in ensuring that part of their best includes inculcating their children with the idea and practice of thinking for themselves. Otherwise, it is possible such children could grow into adults whose ability to think for themselves is greatly diminished. Such children could become adults who rely on being told what to do or adults who fail to appreciate the significance of being able to think for themselves.

Even as adults we still make mistakes sometimes, although we are supposed to be wiser and matured and so should know better, and often when that happens we are corrected using one of many means. For instance, the judiciary aims to correct, and possibly rehabilitate, wrong behaviours in adults. The implication here is that mistakes are unavoidable and could occur even in adults.

I, therefore, reason that if adults, despite their maturity and apparent wisdom, can still make mistakes, necessitating that their actions are constantly monitored by the relevant authorities, then children should be allowed some degree of latitude in their exercise of independent thinking while ensuring that they are equally closely monitored by adults to ensure their safety and protection. We simply shouldn't prevent children from exercising an independent use of their minds for the simple reason that they might make mistakes or come up with wrong decisions if even adults also make mistakes and wrong decisions. An important expected gain from this practice could be children who would be able to think independently, which I suppose is greater in significance than any associated costs (e.g. time spent in correcting errors and mistakes made by children as they are encouraged and allowed to independently reason for themselves).

Incidentally, this controlling attitude is not limited to the family unit or system as it seems to be also prevalent in our educational system. And so, again, having already been exposed to an unhealthy level of mind control or mind-conditioning at home, where the independence and independent use of our minds are largely under-appreciated, we would yet experience more mind-controlling and conditioning as we progress further in life and become part of the world's educational system.

From the lowest branches of our educational system to the highest we are exposed to a type of regimented lifestyle — of rules, regulations, codes of conduct, acceptable practices, ethics, etc. — behind real and imaginary walls and boundaries. We are presented with conditions we are simply expected to comply with. We are not expected to question any of these conditions nor are we expected to ask why they are there.

We are simply expected to do as told — control.

Anyone who protests any of these conditions is labelled a rebel or a deviant and could face one form of punishment or another which have been put in place to ensure compliance. Compliance seems to be the reigning order as it also seems to be the primary thing.

Even the contents of our schools curricula are preset and more or less imposed on us. We are all thought the same things with little or no recognition or regard for our unique individualities. Where we are permitted some degree of choice, with respect to careers or specific areas of study, such choices are not only limited but also preset. It would appear the general assumption is that we are relatively all similar. The implication here is that by limiting our choices our individual uniqueness is ignored. Similarly, expecting us to adapt to existing preset curricula somewhat inhibits our independence as we are unable to freely exercise our desires since we couldn't really pursue studies outside the standard curricula. Since our educational system is not bespoke it would seem that we are simply expected to adapt to the status quo.

Which is another form of doing as told — control.

Please note that I am not trying to criticise our educational system (I suppose it might be practically impossible trying to operate a bespoke academic system) but that, again, all I am trying to do is to point out how our lives could've been influenced by it, just as we have also been influenced by the various other systems we are also exposed to.

Children brought up under the influence of a family system and an educational system that allow for a limited independent expression — at home our parents try to think for us, while the school system also tends to do the same — would possibly end up largely dependent upon external guidance or control. Such children risk growing up not knowing how to use their minds independently or simply might not be used to the practice of thinking for themselves as a matter of default habit.

Consequently, the minds of such children risk being largely under external controls in one form or another. The extended effect would be people who live a life of "do-as-told" and who possibly could become heavily dependent on being told what to do.

What has been demonstrated here is that — because of the nature and mechanisms of the systems of the world we live in — we are from early childhood subjected to many forms of control which greatly impact on an independent application of our minds. Unfortunately, as we progress into adulthood we continue to be constantly exposed and subjected to many other forms of control (most of them institutional) most of which inhibit independent thinking and do not encourage the practice of independent thinking. Consequently, and ultimately, the overall effect is that even as adults we often still fail to engage our minds in the way we rightly should — independently — probably because it is a practice we are not used to since right from home and all through our growing up we are largely expected to exist in compliance as we are expected to be in compliance with set standards.

Be that as it may, a free mind — one solely under our control — is a vital necessity. And one we must all strive to attain. Consequently, although we might've, again, become victims of our circumstances as a result of our upbringing we do not have to remain victims for ever. We could and should take the necessary steps required to bring our victimhood in this particular regard to an end — we need to set our minds free and get them reactivated from their dormant states.

Do recall that I earlier made a demonstration that was aimed at positing that life is essentially in the mind. It means then that a controlled mind would almost always result in a controlled life — with a mind largely under the control of external factors a person is more likely to live not the life they should've lived (or that was intended for them) but the life influenced or orchestrated by such mundane external factors.

- Being able to live the lives we ought to live should be enough motivation to inspire us to set our minds free from all forms of external control.

Similarly, it was pointed out in a previous chapter that for us to live fulfilled lives it is important and necessary we know who we truly are. Consequently, it was suggested that we endeavour to try understanding who we truly are by looking inwards and having an honest conversation with ourselves.

Now such a frank conservation with self would definitely require the application of our minds — thinking is one of the most effective ways we converse with ourselves and probably the only way. Thinking or conversing with ourselves using a mind under any form of external control would largely be ineffective — we are likely to think as guided or coached by such external influences. Consequently, the outcome of a conversation with self which is externally influenced is likely to yield poor results unlike one conducted void of external influences. With a mind under external influences we are unlikely to discover our true identities.

But remember: we need to know who we truly are if we are to live a fulfilled life.

- The desire to live a fulfilled life should be another strong motivation for us to pursue an independent mind.

It was also pointed out in a different chapter that our existence is necessitated by a reason — our purpose — because we are created as a result of the roles we have to play in the world.

Our overall purpose (representing a plurality) is in-built. It is deposited deep inside our inner beings or spirits. To access our purpose would require a great degree of independence — no one else could possibly tell us what our purpose in life is. It then means we need to be in full control of our minds if we are to discover the various reasons we are born.

Inventions, innovations, and other forms of originalities can only be possible where people engage their minds independently. A guided mind or a mind under external influences is not likely to come up with something new — mainly because to come up with new ideas we have to "think outside the box". Thinking outside the box would require an independent mind. It is by thinking outside the box that inventions are possible. Thinking outside the box gave cause to the invention of telephones, cars, trains, aeroplanes, computers, internet, etc. Thinking outside the box also made possible various works of art, books (fiction and non-fiction), fields of study, etc. It is possible these and many other inventions wouldn't have been possible had their inventors confined or limited their thinking to their current statuses quo. Some things — new ideas — were deposited in them and they were able to bring those to actualisation because they dared to apply their minds independently.

It is possible there are many new inventions yet to be actualised but only because the minds they are deposited in are not yet free — they are limited by external influences. It is also possible some inventions may not see the light of day because those who should bring them to existence have failed to use their minds independently.

Not knowing why we are here would mean we may not accomplish the reasons we are here for. Not fulfilling the reasons we are here for could mean an unaccomplished life.

- Being able to accomplish our various purposes should be another strong motivation to set our minds free from any forms of control.

Is your mind free? Or is your mind under any form of control?

Do you believe your thinking process is completely void of external influences? Are your thoughts entirely yours and original? Do you always do what you ought to do? Or do you do only as told? Do you rely or depend on being told what to do? Are you your own person?

If you may, please do conscientiously reflect on these questions and also do a critical review of your life. It may surprise you to realise that you are not entirely in control of your mind as you may wish to think. We are largely products of the system — the system we created. We are products of our families, schools, communities, religious institutions, and our societies in general. We are products of everything we are part of.

It is possible we are subjected to more controls than we could imagine. It is possible we often think as expected, not as we ought to. It is possible our choices are not entirely ours. It is possible the opinions we uphold are inherited or acquired. It is possible our sense of right or wrong is guided or defined by external factors, not personal convictions. It is possible some of the things you have accepted as facts are not facts but fabrications.

Consider the following scenarios:

- Some information is presented to you, say, via mass media, government pamphlets or other publications, or by some institutions: what is your immediate reaction? — Do you simply accept such information to be true? Do you at any time try to verify its veracity? Do you simply believe it solely for its source?
- Some information is presented to you, say, at home, local community, or by friends, about people from a different part of the world as yourself: how do you treat such information? — Do you immediately believe what you have been told? Do you form an opinion about the people in question based simply and wholly on what you have heard? Do you begin to treat the affected people differently?
- You are exposed to a commercial advertisement about a particular product: what is your reaction? — Do you immediately believe in the truthfulness of the advert? Do you instantly form an opinion about the product based solely on the advert (without having even tried it)? Does your opinion about rival products change (even where you have tried and tested them and proven them to be good)?

These are very limited examples but they would suffice in helping to demonstrate the many ways our minds could be brought under different undue external influences.

As powerful as the mind is it is very fragile.

Our minds can easily be subdued by constantly exposing them to a particular thing. What you continue to feed your mind is what it will project by way of thoughts, thoughts then lead to actions. If you are presented with an information and you simply accept it, whether such information is correct or not, you have simply but unwittingly subjected yourself under the influence of that information (and possibly its source). The same principle applies to anything (e.g. ideas, ideologies, concepts, beliefs, etc.) we expose our minds to, especially continuous and prolonged exposures — such things effectively exercise some degree of control over our minds.

To underline the fragile nature of our minds the Bible instructs accordingly:

> Keep your heart with all diligence; for out of it are the issues of life. (Proverbs 4:23; KJV)

And so because our minds are very powerful but at the same time very fragile, we need to exercise due diligence in ensuring that we allow our minds to be exposed to only things that are true, healthy, productive, useful, helpful, and beneficial. We need to ensure that we protect our minds from negative and damaging influences.

The need to apply our minds in thinking, and thinking independently, couldn't be overemphasized. It is only by independently engaging our minds that we are able to discover things for ourselves including the truth about our individual existence.

A complacent attitude towards the rightful use of our minds could be very costly. Adolf Hitler is alleged to have made the following statement:

> "How fortunate for leaders that men do not think"

Imagine that! If you needed a wakeup call I guess this statement alone should do.

The good news is that even if your mind has been subjected to various forms of control it is possible to still set it free. You can set your mind free and bring it under your sole control. To do that you need to first empty your mind of present wrong ideologies, some of which might've been acquired from your upbringing, and then refilling your mind with fresh and positive ideologies by thinking, and thinking independently.

I believe that we all possess an inherent ability to know what is right and what is wrong, it is something which is naturally in-built in every human. It is often when we allow ourselves to be externally influenced that our judgements could be impaired and in such cases we often observe that there is a silent and subtle struggle inside us as we are persuaded to accept wrongs as rights. Sometimes we may know that something is wrong but because either we are compelled to or because of other forms of external pressures (e.g. societal and peer) we might accept that thing to be right against our own conscience. It is such gradual erosion of our conscience which ultimately renders us vulnerable to many wrong ideologies.

However, if and when we decide to reclaim our minds we would once again be able to distinguish between wrongs and rights, and by using our minds independently we would be able to maintain only healthy, positive, and productive mindsets. We would then be able to extricate ourselves from the strong grip of the various systems of the world which have made us victims in more than a few ways — we can end all our victimhoods, inflicted upon us as a result of the systems of the world that we have been a part of or party to.

If you desire to be free: THINK! If you desire a fulfilled life: THINK!

Chapter 7

Love and relationships

The love and relationships we shall be exploring here are not limited to only romantic ones. We shall be looking at relationships holistically — every arrangement or interaction that could qualify as a form of relationship. Simply put, this chapter focuses on how we relate with one another regardless of the nature and constitution of such relationships.

Considering the general nature of human existence, it seems rather obvious we couldn't simply exist in absolute isolation, not needing or having to interact with other people. It is almost impossible that anybody could live without having to interact or relate with some other people in the course of his or her entire life. Since an interaction or relationship with other people is almost a necessity in the course of our existence, it then follows that we couldn't possibly avoid having to relate with other people in one form or another as we pass through life.

Consequently, since an interaction with others is a must, it becomes necessary as well as very important to ensure our interactions or relationships with others are conducted in a right and proper manner. A right and proper relationship with others is a vital necessity because our relationships somehow affect the quality of our lives — good relationships benefit us greatly while bad ones could affect us drastically.

Having established that a relationship with others is a must, and having also pointed out that relationships have to be right and proper it is now necessary for us to determine how best to ensure our relationships are right, proper, and beneficial.

This is where love comes in.

In the absence of love it would almost be impossible conducting relationships in a right and proper manner. Love enables us to treat others as we ought to and it also guarantees maximum benefits from our relationships. Before we can relate with others in love, however, we must first love ourselves, simply because we cannot give what we don't have. It is only when we treat ourselves with love that we are able to treat others with love. Similarly, it is necessary we treat others the same ways we treat ourselves and with the same type of love we have for ourselves. Love cannot be fragmented — whereby it is broken into parts of different proportions and intensities — and can only exist in a wholesome state.

Having established the need for love in our interactions or relationships, let us now reflect on contemporary perception and conception of love.

It would seem love is one of the most subjective concepts in our world — love seems to be severally defined by different people and acquires different meanings under different circumstances. A single person could define love to mean different things depending on circumstances. For instance, we could define the affection we have for close family members as love and we could also define the feeling we have for a romantic interest as love. We could even describe our many interests and preoccupations (e.g. hobbies, pets, material possessions, etc.) as things we love.

And so you can see that our idea of love could be rather ambiguous and at times even confusing. As a result of this ambiguity, love is often misused and abused. Consequently, love often fails to achieve what is should've achieved — largely because of its misapplication.

Love, however, is a vital necessity and so should not be undermined through wrong definitions or understandings, nor rendered unproductive or even counterproductive through misuses or abuses.

In my opinion, love is the centre of our existence because without it living would become almost impossible — we depend on love for most of the things we do in life. It is rather unfortunate then that love is greatly misunderstood, misapplied, and abused.

And so, what is the true meaning of love?

Without going into standard definitions of love, I will say I believe love to mean: doing unto others as you would expect others to do unto you. In my opinion, this is the principle that should govern all human relationships or interactions. I actually believe it is a responsibility — our duty — to treat others as we expect them to treat us. I believe we owe it to each other.

Why?

Simply because, as a matter of fact, we all are different parts of a single whole. We all are related and connected together — and so what affects one person ultimately would affect everybody. Furthermore, we all have the same origin, a fact which has been illustrated in Genesis 1:27, 28 (KJV):

> So God created man in his own image, in the image of God created he him; male and female created he them. And God blessed them, and God said unto them, Be fruitful, and multiply, and replenish the earth, and subdue it: and have dominion over the fish of the sea, and over the fowl of the air, and over every living thing that moveth upon the earth.

We all descended from the same set of fore-parents — the first man and woman commonly referred to as Adam and Eve.

Life

Considering the many differences observable within humanity at large — skins pigmentation, physical builds, languages, etc. — the fact that we are all from the same set of primary parents might seem far-fetched.

I will now try to explain some of these differences — what they are and how they came about.

The origin of diversity in human languages.

Mankind originally had a single language — "And the whole earth was of one language, and of one speech." (Genesis 11:1; KJV) — and which was subsequently diversified — "Go to, let us go down, and there confound their language, that they may not understand one another's speech." (Genesis 11:7; KJV).

The reason for the diversification of our languages has to do with mankind's rebellion against God because it was in order to check this rebellion that our language was diversified into many languages. (More details can be found in Genesis 11: 1 - 9.)

And so the diversity in human languages is an act of God.

The diversity in the physical features.

The first thing to point out here is that even amongst siblings differences still do exist in individual physical features (e.g. sizes, heights, facial impressions, structures, etc.). Although siblings may share a few common features (physical and behavioural), no two individuals are fully identical. We are made in unique ways each with unique features and characteristics.

Similarly, it is possible that people from particular groupings (e.g. ethnicities, tribes, nationalities, etc.) may share a few common traits but this, however, doesn't make them homogeneous as a few individual differences still exist within such groups of people. As a matter of fact, some traits generally attributed to a particular group of people have been found to be present in some individuals from a different grouping, a situation which somehow further emphasises our individual uniqueness.

I believe God made each of us the way we are and although we may all have different qualities and attributes (including physical) that fact doesn't mean we have different origins.

The diversity in skin pigmentation.

The differences in our skins pigmentation have been explained by several scientific and archaeological studies and findings.

The term "race" — denoting a particular group of people — is largely defined based on skin pigmentation. Race — based on skin pigmentation — however, is a misnomer because the whole of humanity share the same origin. And so, effectively, there is only one race — the human race. Which seems to be the findings of studies carried out under the Human Genome Project (HGP) and also the opinion expressed in an editorial based on a research study by Linda Beckerman — which in part stated that it has been "unequivocally determined that there is the same amount of genetic variation among individuals within a so-called racial group as there is between individuals in different racial groups. What that means is there are no real genetic differences between the so-called blacks and the so-called whites, or between either of the two and Asians, or between any of the other so-called races." (Linda Beckerman, PhD; A Paler Shade of Black).

To properly understand how we came about our different skin pigmentation we shall delve briefly into history.

- A brief history of the origin of mankind:

The so-called "modern man" have been shown through historical and archaeological studies to have originated in sub-Saharan Africa. It is also believed these early humans had darker skins or the so-called black skin. Amongst these early humans are also believed to be "Albinos" — people with a partial or complete absence of pigmentation in their skins, hairs, or eyes, due to a lack or deficiency in melanin production.

Subsequently, there was a first wave of migration (outwards or out of Africa, and eastwards) along the coast of Asia, and across the Indian Ocean into the Australian continent, and subsequently into present-day South America.

There was a latter wave of migration (also eastwards) this time using an inland route through Southern Asia up to present-day China before these migrants settled in Central Asia, and subsequently journeying on to Northern Asia. It is believed the lightening of the darker skin could've occurred sometime during this phase of early human migration. The primary reason behind the lightening of skins has been scientifically attributed to prolonged exposure to colder temperate climates with lower ultra violet (UV) rays from the sunshine in these areas.

Different geographical areas are exposed to different levels of UV rays and lower UV levels in the sunlight of the more northern latitudes would probably have necessitated natural adaptation and gene mutations that could've led to a lighter skin. Low UV rays meant that an individual's body could not produce enough Vitamin D — which assists the human body in the production and maintenance of melanin. Melanin is the chief ingredient responsible for the darker skin colour (or black skin) and a deficiency in melanin would naturally result in a lighter skin. Low UV rays would mean insufficient vitamin D, insufficient vitamin D would lead to a deficiency in the production of melanin by the body, and a deficiency in melanin would result in lighter skins. (It has also been suggested in some quarters that interbreeding between the darker early humans and their albino counterparts might've also somehow contributed to the lightening of the skins of subsequent generations. In support of this theory, instances were sighted of present-day offspring of similar interbreeding — between dark-skinned people and albinos — which seem to have resulted in light-skinned babies. Further details about these latter occurrences — and also about the history of the black and albino people of Asia — can be found at: realhistoryww.com/world_history/ancient/China_2.htm.)

It means the differences in our skins pigmentation is possibly largely due to natural or environmental factors.

Any detailed study of human origins would reveal a single primary ancestry.

A very significant implication here is that most differentiating classifications and categorisation (e.g. races, nationalities, ethnicities, tribes, etc.) are entirely superficial and man-made.

Mankind is one but we have divided ourselves into various parts based on real or imaginary differences. Incidentally, these divisions have done us more harm than good. I could suggest that these divisions are our biggest problems because many problems we face in the world today can all be traced to one form of division or another.

I will like to highlight some of these problems for the simple reason of using them to buttress the point that most of our problems are largely due to divisions based on real or imaginary differences.

Slavery.

Oftentimes when people make reference to historic slavery it usually is in reference to the transatlantic slavery which occurred between mid-fifteenth century and late-nineteenth century. Slavery, however, has been in practice long before transatlantic slavery. The practice has also continued (howbeit in different covert forms) up to present times.

Below is a summary timeline of historic slavery:

- 6800 BC: The world's first city-state emerges in Mesopotamia. Land ownership and the early stages of technology bring war — in which enemies are captured and forced to work as slaves.
- 2575 BC: Temple art celebrate the capture of slaves in battle. Egyptians capture slaves by sending special expeditions up the Nile River.

- 550 BC: The city-state of Athens uses as many as 30,000 slaves in its silver mines.
- 120 AD: Roman military campaigns capture slaves by the thousands. Some estimate the population of Rome is more than half slave.
- 500 AD : Anglo-Saxons enslave the native Britons after invading England.
- 1000 AD: Slavery is a normal practice in England's rural, agricultural economy, as destitute workers place themselves and their families in a form of debt bondage to landowners.
- 1380: In the aftermath of the Black Plaque, Europe's slave trade thrives in response to a labour shortage. Slaves pour in from all over the continent, the Middle East, and North Africa.
- 1444: Portuguese traders bring the first large cargo of slaves from West Africa to Europe by sea — establishing the Atlantic slave trade.
- 1526: Spanish explorers bring the first African slaves to settlements in what would become the United States. These first African Americans stage the first known slave revolt in the Americas.
- 1550: Slaves are depicted as objects of conspicuous consumption in much Renaissance art.
- 1641: Massachusetts becomes the first British colony to legalize slavery.

It is instructive to note from the above timeline that the first recorded account of slavery arose from a war situation — circa 6800 BC — where the captured prisoners of war were used as slaves. What this demonstrates is that slavery was occasioned by a type of division — and the warring parties belonged to different groups.

A review of any particular slave practice would most likely reveal it was either occasioned by one form of division or another, or it was facilitated as a result of similar divisions — slavery is often a "we-against-them" scenario, which could be based on skin colour, nationality, ethnicity, or even social status or class.

Colonisation.

Colonisation — imposition of dominant rule by one party on another — is fraught with many atrocities. For a start, it is a gross violation of the natural rights of the people colonised. In my opinion, colonisation is very much the same as slavery.

A brief history of colonisation is presented below:

- Modern state global colonisation — or imperialism — began in the fifteenth century with the Age of Discovery led by Portuguese and Spanish exploration of the Americas, and the coasts of Africa, the Middle East, India and East Asia.
- During the sixteenth and seventeenth centuries, England, France and the Dutch Republic established their own overseas empires, in direct competition with each other.
- The end of the eighteenth century and early nineteenth century saw the first era of decolonisation when most of the European colonies in the Americas gained their independence from their respective metropoles or colonial masters.
- Spain was irreversibly weakened after the loss of their New World colonies but the Kingdom of Great Britain, France, Portugal, and the Dutch turned their attention to the Old World, particularly South Africa, India, Pakistan and South East Asia where coastal enclaves had already been established.
- The second industrial revolution — in the nineteenth century led to what has been termed the era of New Imperialism — when the pace of colonisation rapidly accelerated, the height of which was the Scramble for Africa in which Belgium, Germany and Italy were participants.
- During the twentieth century, the colonies of the losers of World War I were distributed amongst the victors as mandates, but it was not until the end of World War II (around the mid-twentieth century) that the second phase of decolonisation began in earnest.

The negative consequences of colonisation have widely been acknowledged both by victims and perpetrators. The main objective here is to simply point out that colonisation was possible mainly as a result of the "we against them" mentality.

Holocaust.

Holocaust here, is in reference to the genocide of the Jews — mainly in Europe — systematically carried out by Adolf Hitler's Nazi regime — the Third Reich — and its collaborators.

It is estimated a total of approximately six million Jews were directly killed as a result of the Holocaust. Some historians also include the additional, approximately, five million non-Jewish victims of Nazi mass murders as part of the Holocaust. Taking into account, however, all of the victims of Nazi-related persecutions, it is estimated about seventeen million people — Jews and non-Jews — were killed as a result of the Holocaust.

The bottom line here is that about seventeen million people lost their lives and properties, in a relatively short period of time, simply because they were considered different.

Genocides or Ethnic cleansings.

Our world has witnessed several genocides or so-called ethnic cleansings in its history. There was the Armenian Genocide — during which the Ottoman government, after World War I (sometime in April 1915), systematically exterminated its minority Armenian population to an estimated tune of 800,000 - 1.5 million people inside their historic homeland which lies within the territory constituting the present-day Republic of Turkey.

There was also the Rwandan Genocide — when the Hutu majority, in approximately one hundred days (between April 7th and July 15th 1994) wiped out between 500,000 - 1,000,000 fellow Rwandans simply because they belonged to another ethnic group, Tutsi.

Genocides are a good example of the negative consequences of divisions — in this case divisions into different ethnic groups. A multitude of people are targeted and killed only because they are deemed to be different.

Wars.

Almost every warfare that have been fought in the history of mankind — including World Wars I and II — have been fought on the basis of perceived differences between the warring factions. Sometimes these differences are so insignificant or simplistic they often are irrelevant.

Imagine how many people were senselessly killed during World Wars I and II. Imagine the countless others that have died due to one warfare or another. In addition to loss of human lives, also imagine how much humanity has lost to different warfare — natural resources, properties, natural heritages, etc.

Now, consider that those losses were largely due to divisions based on perceived differences.

Sad, right?

Famines, Diseases, Poverties and other acts of Mass Destruction.

It is arguable famines, diseases and poverties prevalent in a particular part of the world may not have directly resulted from the actions of people in other parts of the world — although in most cases they are.

Many times some regions of the world are impoverished as a result of exploitations by people from other regions. In other instances, some parts of the world are impoverished or still suffer deprivations (in one form or another) as a consequence of their past (e.g. slavery, colonisation, wars, etc.). In addition to these direct causes, neglects or inactions on the part of the unaffected regions also indirectly contribute in helping to perpetuate problems like famines, diseases, poverties, earthquakes, landslides, etc. Exploitations, marginalisation, discriminations, and neglect are all largely due to perceived differences. People are often exploited or neglected because they are deemed different.

These examples are very limited but they will suffice in demonstrating that most of the problems we have in the world are largely due to our perceived differences.

The biggest irony, however, is that we are not different — we are all the same and have the same primary origin. More so, we are all interconnected as different parts of a single whole. Consequently, when we treat another person wrongly we are inadvertently also treating ourselves wrongly. Which is why I pointed out earlier that relating with other people in the right and proper manner is a duty — a responsibility — and something we owe ourselves.

It is possible that you have unwittingly imbibed this destructive negative mindset — the "we-against-them" mentality — or that you were simply brought up believing in some of the differences based on which humanity has been dissected and diversified.

It is possible that you believe you ought to protect yourself from and against those you believe to be the "them". It is also possible you see nothing wrong in treating those you consider different, differently. It may be you have operated (or is still operating) a system of double-standards — where a set of rules apply to you (and your likes) while another set of rules apply to the others.

It is possible you believe you are different and better. It is also possible that you harbour an obscure disdain for those you deem different.

It is possible you do all of these without even realising you are doing so. It is possible you are completely unaware that you have this mindset and it is possible you believe it to be natural and normal.

And so it is possible that in loving you only show love to a select few — those in your "we" circle.

But is there really a "we" and a "them"? Let us see.

Please consider the following scenarios:

- In the family system we have our nuclear family as part of an extended family structure. Since our nuclear family is "different" from the other nuclear families in our extended family: do the other nuclear families qualify as "them"? Should it be "we" — members of our nuclear family — against "them" — members of the other nuclear families in our extended family?
- In cultures that recognise villages or hamlets our extended families form part of a collection of extended families which make up our villages or hamlets. Since other extended families in our villages are "different" from our extended family: are those other extended families to be regarded as "them"? Are all the families in our extended family to be regarded as "we"?

(Did you notice any inconsistency? How a previous "them" — other families in our extended family — could now become or qualify as a "we" because, relative to other extended families, members of our extended family are considered same as us.)

- In the so-called racial classification there are blacks and there are whites. Within each broad group of black or white there are other sub-groups — apparently there are different types of blacks as there are different types of whites.

And so within the "black race", for instance, there are blacks from Africa and there are blacks from Australia: are the African blacks different from Australian aborigines? Can one group qualify as a "we" and the other a "them" since they are "different"?

Lets now see what happens when blacks are considered together as a single group.

- This time we have all the black people in one group as black race and all the white people in another as white race: should all black people (Africans and Australian aborigines inclusive) regard themselves as a "we" while all white people regarded themselves as "them"?

(Notice that inconsistency again?)

- In some countries (e.g. United States of America and South Africa) there are ethnic white populations as well as ethnic black populations. If United States of America is pitched against South Africa: would the ethnic white populations in both countries regard themselves as a "we"? Will the ethnic black populations in both countries qualify as a "them" to the whites in the two countries?

It is more than likely that both white and black Americans will unite against black and white South Africans, and vice versa. What then happened to the earlier consideration of all blacks as "we" and all whites as "them"?

As limited as these examples are at least they suffice in exposing the inconsistencies and pettiness that characterise the many classifications we have, most of which are based on superficial or imaginary differences and not forgetting that these divisive classifications are grossly irrelevant too and unnecessary in the first place.

So do you believe there is a "we" and a "them"? Maybe not. Or maybe.

Please reflect upon the following questions:

- Do you regard your family members as different from the rest of the world's population? Would you treat family and non-family equally and alike?
- Do you make friends only of people who are similar to you in most ways? Are you cautious of people who might appear different in appearance to yourself?

- Have you already formed an opinion about a particular group of people who might look different to the way you look? Do you stereotype people based on their origins or backgrounds?
- Are you more inclined to helping those you consider similar to yourself? Are you relatively indifferent to the plights of others who appear different to you in appearance?
- Do you consider yourself a patriot, whose sworn allegiance is for a particular country? Are you partisan in any way, with a strong and partial support for a particular cause, group or people?
- Do you believe some people should be entitled to certain privileges which others shouldn't? As an employer would you employ jobseekers strictly and only based on individual merit and qualifications? Would you offer opportunities to all on an equal-basis?
- Do you believe some people are better than others?
- Would you treat others just as you would expect to be treated?

Just a few question, but your answers would reveal a lot about you.

It may surprise you to know that there are possibly more people who believe in the "we" and "them" syndrome than don't. It may also surprise you that a majority of those who do are completely unaware they do.

Recall that at the beginning of the chapter it was pointed out that we couldn't possibly pass through life without having to relate with other people. It was also suggested we must relate with others in the right and proper manner — effectively, how we would expect others to relate with us. It was then demonstrated that by treating others in the right and proper manner we benefit ourselves — since our relationships have a significant impact on our lives.

It means then that if we want a better life we have to ensure our relationships or interactions with others — every one of them — are conducted in line with that golden rule: doing unto others how you would want others to do unto you.

How you have conducted your relationships in the past might not be as relevant as how you decide to conduct them going forward — you may actually learn a few lessons from the past that could be applied in the present in order to guarantee a better future.

Now is the beginning of your future — the rest of your life.

But remember: a good life could depend on how good you treat others.

Chapter 8

Money rules

It is often said that money rules the world: with money almost anything is possible. This seems to be a widely accepted maxim and one which is upheld my many. Popular culture seems to suggest that money is everything and so should be acquired at all cost. It also seems to equate a successful life to an abundance of material possessions — money equals success and to be successful is to have an abundance of money.

Similarly, some people wrongly believe that having more money would guarantee happiness.

It may well be that such popular opinions or beliefs are not without a basis since a particular verse in the Bible seems to express a similar sentiment:

> A feast is made for laughter, and wine maketh merry: **but money answereth all things**. (Ecclesiastes 10:19; KJV)

Is money everything though? Is it possible money is the answer to all things?

Whatever the correct answers are to these questions they do not change the fact that many people do believe in the supremacy of money, and that it is a type of panacea. Consequently, it is very likely people brought up in societies (or in a world) where money is regarded as all-important and a must-have would grow up with such mindsets. They would believe that money is everything and with such a belief such people are likely to live as though money is all-important and a must-have. As a result such people are likely to live a life driven essentially by the desire to acquire money in abundance — money could become their main or only motivation in life. And so right from an early age such people could invest all of their resources (e.g. time, energy, abilities, etc.) in the insatiable quest for the illusive wealth — they could lay their all on the altar of money, as it were.

The problem though is that money is not everything, and it isn't the only thing either. As a matter of fact, money is primarily just a means to an end. Money is that which we can use in exchange for goods and services, it doesn't qualify as goods or services — money is essentially intangible. Similarly, money has little or no intrinsic value — on its own money is practically worthless — but it acquires value only when exchanged for goods or services. For instance, a ten-dollar bill is worthless, as a piece of paper, whereas a pair of jeans could be worth ten dollars. It means the value of the ten-dollar bill is the pair of jeans it could be used in exchange for.

What this simple illustration demonstrates is that money, matter-of-factly, instead of being everything is actually nothing. It shows that what has value (and hence important) are those things we need, and for which we require money for their purchase. It means a million dollars stashed away in a hideout has no value unless and until it is used in exchange for something tangible that has value. Otherwise it is just a massive bundle of paper.

A simple deduction then is that striving tirelessly for more money is simply striving tirelessly for more bundles of paper which on its own is effectively worthless.

The overall implication, therefore, is that what we should really concern ourselves with are our needs (as against wants) and not money — we ought to focus more on our needs and not the means with which we could satisfy them (money). And so it is very important we carefully identify our needs, using them as our main motivation in our daily endeavours (i.e. we aim to provide for our needs) otherwise we risk labouring excessively for more than we need (i.e. striving for an excess or a surplus).

Is it prudent to accumulate surpluses? Is it sensible to exert ourselves only to be left with more than we needed? Should we deny ourselves a simpler life in order to accumulate excesses we may not utilise in our lifetime?

Without first identifying our needs it is possible we could engage in many unnecessary and avoidable endeavours, and at great personal costs too. We may even end up labouring in vain. I would suppose a better approach to life would be to first establish our needs before trying to provide for them. In other words our acquisitions (including our quest for money) ought to be need-based. That way our efforts would be commensurate with our rewards — as we would've laboured for only what we needed, and not labouring for more than we need. Surpluses are not necessarily rewarding, especially when the opportunity costs (what we had to forgo) of such surpluses are taken into account.

It means then that we shouldn't simply aspire to be millionaires, for instance, if our needs can well be catered for with less than millions. It takes more efforts to make millions and so it might not be worthwhile tasking ourselves to make millions only to be left in the end with excess money.

As sound as the above logic may be, however, fact is we often live a life of excessive endeavours largely driven by the desire for more (especially more money) — this seems to be the status quo.

Almost as soon as we are born we begin to be prepared for a successful life — as defined by popular culture. Our upbringing, education, choices of career, choices of employment, grooming, choices of lifestyle, etc. are all largely influenced and driven by a single objective — success in life. We are taught to be ambitious, are enrolled in particular academic institutions, counselled to pursue particular careers, encouraged to seek employment in particular fields and with particular companies or organizations, expected to adopt particular lifestyles, encouraged to choose particular marital partners, encouraged to have particular family sizes, etc. all so we can accomplish that single objective of a successful life. Which is all very good but only if our definition of success is the right one.

The overall result is that without even being aware of it, we embark on the journey of life with a mindset that regards money as all-important and a must-have. Money becomes everything to us, as it were, and so we pursue it relentlessly (and almost blindly).

It often is the case that even before we attain the legal working age we are already engaged in some form of labour or another with money usually our primary motivation. We may engage in part-time and temporary employments not because our basic needs are not been met by those responsible for us but in order to satisfy our private indulgences. We may work to fund a lifestyle we have chosen, and possibly one influenced by peer pressure or popular culture. We may desire every latest gizmos, trending fashions, or other lifestyles which might be beyond our ordinary means and most of which may not rightly constitute our true needs, hence we may be expected to provide for them ourselves. As a result we involve ourselves in premature labour often earlier than necessary. Consequently, from an early age we consciously expose ourselves to a life of excessive stress and, sometimes, strife.

Remember: such premature vocational preoccupations could greatly affect the quality of our young lives, and that they could be avoided.

As we progress in life it's often the case that we continue to desire and aspire for more than we need. We continue to indulge in the things we want even though we might not need them. Here, again, peer and societal pressures as well as popular culture seem to be our biggest influencer.

We may wish to live in particular neighbourhoods, buy or rent particular types of houses, buy particular cars (sometimes more cars than we actually need), enrol in particular social or sports clubs, take up subscription or membership with particular institutions or organizations, furnish our houses with state-of-the-art gizmos or equipment, adopt particular lifestyles, and indulge in various other things only so as to present ourselves as successful individuals especially since we believe such choices to represent a successful living.

And so we may labour excessively in order to afford our choices which effectively might not comprise only of our needs.

A big irony is that some people in order to afford a particular lifestyle, labour tirelessly so much so that in the end they are unable to enjoy the lifestyle they have exerted themselves so greatly for. For instance, some people may wish to be current and up-to-date with latest technologies and so might keep upgrading their gizmos to the latest models even where they rarely utilise most of the new features. Similarly, some people may like to acquire every gizmos out there although they rarely use most of them. Some may have full cable-TV subscriptions but are rarely at home to enjoy the services provided (possibly because they have to now work more in order to pay for such subscriptions) and so are effectively labouring in vain for an acquisition they couldn't properly enjoy. Some enrol with gyms or other fitness centres (mostly as a status-symbol) but rarely utilise the services provided. Some buy large houses whose many rooms are left unoccupied. Others buy more cars than they can drive. These might all be rightly regarded as wantonness but, sadly, it is not uncommon.

As unnecessary and avoidable as these indulgences in excesses are they are equally very harmful in many ways.

Sometimes having to labour excessively (in order to afford our chosen lifestyles) might deny us useful socialisation or associations — our relationships with other people (e.g. family members, neighbours, people in our various local communities and circles, etc.) could be adversely affected in ways which might render them ineffective and not fit for purpose. It often is the case that some children are denied the right and proper type of parenting because their parents are excessively engaged in their respective careers or employments. Similarly, some marriages suffer because the parties involved fail to make time for each other but instead are more preoccupied with work. Some people find it difficult finding a wife or a husband because they spend more time working ceaselessly that they have no time for meaningful relationships.

Furthermore, working more than is necessary could also directly and adversely impact our personal lives in other ways.

We may fail to properly look after ourselves thereby endangering our health, possibly shortening our lifespan. The quality of our lives might also be greatly diminished — we may live lives full of avoidable stresses and strife — meaning we may fail to enjoy life itself. Sometimes people desire a good life and so they work very hard — life for them becomes work, work and more work — and they work as they commute to work, while at their workplaces, while on break, at home, weekdays and weekends, during public holidays, and some work even while on personal holidays but, sadly, by working very hard they deny themselves the good life they desired in the first place which led them into having to work very hard. Bit of a tragedy.

It is sad that for some people living equates to working and working equates to living but life is much more than mere material possessions and it also is worth more than them.

The life that ought to be is sweet, enjoyable, and simple. Our maker, God, didn't design life to be stressful and the complexity it seems to have become — God created everything else for our benefit and so he obviously intended life to be enjoyable and pleasurable for us. The life we live is essentially the one we have chosen. It is also the one we have made for ourselves.

Life could become stressful when we ignore our needs focusing instead on our wants (or indulgences).

Let us briefly examine life purely from a need-basis:

- The most essential things in life — things without which living would be impossible — are free.

We are created free — we didn't pay for our creation. We didn't even have to request it. And so the ultimate thing in life (life itself) is FREE!

The air we need to remain alive if free — we don't pay for the air we breathe. Without oxygen we could barely stay alive, but it is FREE!

Water is widely available free — rainfall, rivers, seas and oceans are naturally available without cost.

Sunlight — which humans, plants and animals depend on for various forms of sustenance — is free.

Other natural resources — e.g. minerals, vegetations, animals, forests, fisheries and other marine lives, etc., effectively our entire ecosystems — are available free. They are all created (just as we are) and primarily for our benefit. They originally are provided for us free.

Note: Our core needs are provided for us free meaning we don't have to stress for their provision.

- Our basic needs — the fundamental requirements which serve as the foundation for our survival — are relatively cheap and easily affordable.

The foods we need for our survival are relatively cheap in their basic forms. Staple foods in different parts of the world are usually the cheapest foods in their respective localities. Cereals (e.g. wheat, barley, oats, rye, etc.), other grains (e.g. rice, maize, etc.), tubers or root vegetables (e.g. yam, potatoes, cassava, taro, cocoyam, etc.), legumes (e.g. beans, lentils, peas, soybeans, etc.) — most of which are staples in different regions of the world are often the cheapest foods especially in their basic forms. Similarly, animal products and by-products (e.g. milk, cheese, butter, lard, beef, mutton, chicken, eggs, sausages, etc.) are normally locally in abundance and often relatively cheap (again, in their basic forms).

The reality is that most of what constitute our basic dietary requirements — foods we need for our survival — are abundantly available at relatively affordable prices in their basic forms.

Ironically, although these foods are readily available and affordable we have decided to process them in ways that present them as superior or better than their basic forms thereby making them more expensive consequently. And so instead of basic oats we may prefer something made entirely of oats but more expensive. We may also instead of normal chicken opt for a processed product largely made from chicken but that is also more expensive. The overall implication here is that in our wisdom (or lack of it) we have made foods which ordinarily are cheap more expensive for ourselves and we also seem to prefer the more expensive versions, possibly because we believe they make us look more successful or richer than those who use the basic forms of these foods. But the cost of our choices is having to work more in order to earn more so we can afford our choices.

Our shelters could be made available relatively cheaper if they are priced conservatively taking into consideration their actual costs. Sometimes a smaller apartment in one part of a city could be valued far more than a bigger apartment in another part of the same city. Similarly, some houses are built in plots of land that could comfortably accommodate many more houses. Yet some other houses are made more expensive by several aesthetic add-ons some of which have no real or practical value.

Consequently, houses which should have otherwise been easily affordable become unaffordable to many. Incidentally, it would seem that more people also prefer the more expensive parts of particular cities and, in other cases, the more expensive houses, possibly as status-symbols.

(Please note that I am not criticising any of these practices and that I am simply pointing them out to help show how we have complicated what ordinarily could've been simpler.)

The basic clothing we need are relatively cheap — the actual costs of making most clothes are not that high — but we have somehow overwhelmed ourselves with our preferences for very expensive alternatives.

Consequently, some people, who cannot easily afford them, would exert themselves some more in order to acquire designer labels all as status-symbols and evidence of doing well.

Generally-speaking, there is nothing wrong when someone who can easily afford more expensive things chooses to do so. The problem is when someone who cannot easily afford these more expensive versions of particular items prefers them, possibly because he or she believes that acquiring such expensive items would set him or her apart from the rest of the public or would make him or her feel and look successful, and as a result he or she has to work harder than otherwise necessary so as to be able to afford his or her choices.

Note: Our basic needs are readily available in cheaper versions meaning that we don't have to be in possession of too much money to afford them.

What we have shown so far is that most of the things we need for our existence and survival — general essentials and individual basic needs — are either free or relatively cheap meaning that a good life is not as expensive as some of us think it is or make it look. It means we can all enjoy good lives relatively easier than we probably do now.

So why then do some people engage in excessive endeavours including working more than ordinarily necessary?

The simple answer might lie in these two words — needs and wants.

Needs are not the same as wants and wants, on the other hand, are not necessarily needs. When we carefully analyse the things we often desire and for which we aspire, we are likely to realise that a reasonable proportion of these would not qualify as genuine needs. And so it would seem that we oftentimes simply accumulate possessions based on our fancies, and that some of the things we accumulate are not genuine needs. More so, we could also wrongly define our needs (or what we presume to be our needs) largely as a result of wrong influences. We may, for instance, presume we need a particular thing (possibly because most people either already possess that thing or also want it) whereas in reality we have no need for that thing. For instance, we may presume we need the latest version of a handset whereas in reality we don't. We may also presume we need a particular designer handbag, pair of shoes, or wristwatch whereas in reality we don't. We may also presume we need a new car whereas our current car is well ok for our mobility needs. The list could go on but the point is that sometimes the things we classify as needs could actually be mere wants or desires driven largely by ostentation, vanity or ego.

Failing to clearly and correctly distinguish between our needs and our wants could mean our having to task ourselves with more strenuous vocational endeavours than would've been otherwise necessary to ensure a good quality of life or living, which could consequently mean living a lesser quality of life than we could've had had we simply focused mainly on our needs. It could also mean living a less-than-satisfying life.

It is instructive pointing out that our wants are often and mostly influenced or driven by societal pressures and popular cultures — some things are considered status-symbols and as a result most people aspire to have them often as evidence that they have "arrived" or that they "belong". Again, this might be another consequence of a controlled mind where people are made to presume that certain possessions set them apart from the rest of the public and that certain possessions are symbols of success. It means some people might do certain things not because they would've done so otherwise but because they believe they are expected to do so especially so as to validate their social statuses. It also means some people could acquire certain properties only because they presume they make them look successful.

The overall result is that the life we live is largely the one we have chosen. (Sadly, it is not always the best.)

The good news, however, is that since the life we now live is essentially the one we have chosen, we can equally change it by simply deciding to choose a better life especially if we find the current one cumbersome, unsatisfactory, or unfruitful. The easiest way to effect this change, in my opinion, would be to address the mindset (or mindsets) responsible for the life we have chosen — in this particular instance the mindset which regards money as all-important and a must-have.

Before making a change, the first thing, however, would be to first determine whether or not you have this mindset. To help you determine whether you are a victim of this mindset, and by how much, or not try doing the following exercises:

The first is a list of questions which you should attempt answering as truthfully as possible. Taking into consideration the various things already highlighted and discussed in this chapter — Would you say that you believe money is a panacea? Are you largely driven by the need to have more money? Are your needs (or what you presume to be your needs) defined by popular cultures? Are you easily influenced by peer or societal pressures? Do you aspire to appear successful (as defined by general standards)? Do you believe in status-symbols? Do you believe money guarantees happiness? Will you do anything to make money? Do you believe having money in abundance automatically entitles you to certain privileges? Do you believe having money in abundance makes you untouchable? Do you believe money is all-important and a must-have? Does money top your priorities? Do you think it is possible to live a good life without having an abundance of money?

In case you are finding it a bit difficult answering one or more of these questions, maybe the second batch of exercises could provide you with some assistance.

Let us now consider the following scenarios:

- A situation where a man or woman uses his or her body for the purpose of obtaining monetary favours or other benefits in kind. In other words, he or she willingly offers himself or herself for the sexual pleasure of another in direct or indirect exchange for money, gifts or other forms of compensation — it could be done on a purely commercial-basis or through one form of relationship or another but the underlying fact is that material gain is the main motivation.

- A young girl pretends to be in love or in a relationship with a man, mainly or solely for the material benefits such a relationship affords her, meaning that she might have a string of male friends (each of whom she claims to love or to be in a relationship with). Or it could be a young boy in a similar arrangement with a string of female friends.
- A lady sleeps with her best friend's boyfriend or husband mainly for monetary gains or other benefits in kind. Or a man sleeps with his best mate's girlfriend or wife for similar reasons.
- A man makes sexual advances towards a married woman, or any woman at all, applying his wealth as a tool for wooing her, howbeit wrongly. In other words, he believes because he has a lot of money he is either entitled to do as he pleases or that his wealth would make anything possible for him including sleeping with as many women as he pleases or with another man's wife. Or it could be a woman wooing a married man or other men under similar circumstances.
- A man makes sexual advances towards his daughter's female friends or schoolmates using monetary rewards as a means of obtaining their consent. Or it could be a woman under similar circumstances who does same to her son's male friends or schoolmates.
- A man or woman sleeps with a prospective employer in order to secure an employment. Or does same with a boss for a promotion at work or for other benefits.
- A politician accepts a financial inducement or bribe in exchange for political favours.
- A public office-holder (e.g. a national leader, government minister, political appointee, a company director or manager, etc.) embezzles public resources entrusted in his or her care misappropriating them for personal benefits in a case of crass abuse of power and trust.
- A person robs a defenceless old man or woman of his or her possessions.
- A person sheds the blood of another person in a diabolical ritual performed for one purpose or another (e.g. wealth, political power or position, or one form of material advancement or another).

- A person arranges the murder of a political opponent, business rival or partner, or an associate for material benefits.
- A person decides to monetise their annual holidays — by offering to work during his or her holiday period in exchange for more money — instead of enjoying time away from work.
- A person chooses a job he or she knows he or she wouldn't enjoy doing and that he or she ordinarily wouldn't want to do but only because it offers more pay.
- A person is in the habit of buying the latest gizmos not because he or she really uses them but just as status-symbols.

(While some of these decisions or actions are generally misguided and in bad taste, most are downright deplorable and morally unacceptable.)

The task is to now examine yourself whether you have, still do, or would do (if given the opportunity) any of these or similar things.

Any affirmative answers would suggest that you are somehow already a victim of the mindset in question — money rules mindset — but generally-speaking, your answers would determine how much premium you place on material possessions and whether or not you believe money rules, is a must-have-at-all-cost or all-important.

If perhaps you discover that you are indeed a victim of this mindset then it would be necessary and appropriate to make that change after all. Otherwise you might be left stuck with the life you now live which essentially is the one you have chosen. But remember that if you find the life you now live a bit tedious, stressful, unsatisfying, or unfulfilling it can be made better by deciding to change your choices and choosing the life that you ought to be living.

The harmful effects of this negative mindset — of money rules — have already been highlighted — which essentially is that we could drive ourselves more than necessary thereby inadvertently denying ourselves the good life we set out to achieve in the first place. It may also result in a poorer health which could lead to shortening of our lives. Generally-speaking, it could lead to an unfulfilled and unsatisfied life.

Bad enough.

A bigger tragedy, however, is that it is often only at the end of such lives people realise the futility of it all — they then realise it wasn't worth it after all. It is often at life's mortal end some people realise money cannot guarantee happiness, that success is not rightly defined by material achievements alone, or that status-symbols are just vanities — they offer no real satisfaction except that of massaging egos. Sadly, by the time of these realisations it often is too late for the people in question to benefit from them. So that the knowledge now gained is practically of no benefit to those who have directly earned them.

Some wise people say that experience is the best teacher. While I fully agree with them I will like to add…only if we learn from them. Some other wise people say that experience gained is better than experience earned. Again, I fully agree. We gain from the experiences of others while we earn ours. Having to earn from our experiences, however, can be very costly, meaning that it is better, more profitable and wiser to gain from other people's experiences.

And so it would seem that we need a dose of wisdom if we are to navigate through life relatively effortlessly avoiding the many pitfalls along the pathway of life.

- We need to get our priorities in the right order.
- We need to clearly and correctly identify our needs — the things we need for our existence and survival.
- We need to distinguish our needs from our wants.
- We need to focus more on our needs than on our wants.
- We need to live in the now, and although we ought to make plans for the future we must not allow our preoccupation with the future deny us our enjoyment of the present.
- We also need to realise that we are not primarily responsible for our existence — God is, and by deeming it necessary to create us has automatically assumed responsibility for our lives. (More on this later.)

One thing is now obvious and it is that wisdom is a key prerequisite for a successful life.

Wisdom, however, is different from knowledge or intelligence. Wisdom is the application of knowledge, but before we can apply knowledge we must first acquire knowledge.

And what better way could we acquire knowledge than to engage with our maker — almighty God — who knows everything we need to know. It would seem improbable that we could pass through life without having to relate with our maker, just as we probably couldn't live without having to relate with other people. This relationship with our maker, however, is even more significant and more of a necessity than our relationships with other humans.

We shall consider this relationship next.

Chapter 9

Religion

Religion is primarily a relationship between a person and God — in the right and original context it basically is simply that. It comprises the daily interactions (both definite, abstract or subliminal), communications, worships, adorations, devotions, etc., which transpire between a person and God. Simply put, religion is the means by which a person relates with God.

Religion isn't just a set of rules and regulations, a system of personal beliefs, or a collection of creeds or doctrines which demand strict compliances and observances. It also isn't just any random ways we might choose to, seemingly, interact with our maker, God. It is a relationship, and like most relationships there is a right way of conducting it.

The proper way — that right way — by which we might engage God in a relationship has been instituted by God, right from the beginning of creation.

The origin of religion.

The earliest recorded account of an interaction between humans and God is found in Genesis 3:8 (KJV):

> And they heard the voice of the Lord God walking in the garden in the cool of the day: and Adam and his wife hid themselves from the presence of the Lord God amongst the trees of the garden.

Two basic (and vital) facts are presented in the verse above:

- They heard the voice of the Lord God walking in the garden.
- They hid themselves from the presence of the Lord God.

The first — to hear someone — indicates a form of interaction. The second — to hide from someone — also indicates a type of interaction (howbeit somewhat negative in nature).

From these facts a few reasonable deductions could be made:

- It would be reasonable to presume that the people involved — Adam and Eve — were not hearing this voice for the first time.

Hearing the voice and consequently going into hiding strongly suggests that Adam and wife recognised the voice. For both to have recognised the voice would imply a prior acquaintanceship with the voice, they must've heard the voice previously for them to now recognise it.

Consequently, we would be right to conclude there have been previous interactions between Adam, Eve, and the voice of the Lord God.

- It would also seem reasonable to presume that Adam and Eve didn't always hide upon hearing the voice.

The simple fact it was reported that they hid, upon hearing the voice, strongly suggests this particular behaviour to be an exception rather than the norm. I don't suppose it would've been necessary highlighting that they hid if they have always hidden from the voice.

And so we could possibly conclude from the foregoing deductions that Adam and Eve had interactions with the Lord God — implying a relationship of sorts. I believe this to be the origin of religion.

With its origin established, let us now explore the true meaning of religion.

To properly understand what religion truly is we shall look at its main characteristics — its defining elements or features — using this relationship between God, Adam and Eve as a model and guide.

Some main characteristics of religion.

Based on recorded accounts of interactions between God and the first humans — Adam and Eve — the following are what I suppose to be some key features or characteristics of religion:

- It is based on the one true God — the Creator.
- It is instituted by God not by the human party.
- It is a direct relationship between a person and God.
- It is void of rituals, formalities or protocols.
- It is based on truth and sincerity — e.g. Adam and Eve hid upon hearing the voice of the Lord God possibly because they knew they had disobeyed God.

Some key points to note would include: Adam and Eve were not responsible for choosing how best to interact with God (God made himself available to them in ways he chose); the interactions were both direct and personal (there was no use of intermediaries); the absence of strict adherences to rituals, ceremonies, performances, or observances (it was often spontaneous, instantaneous, and was conducted under a liberal but solemn atmosphere); and, lastly, it was frank, sincere, and wholesome.

And so based on the foregoing, I believe religion to be a direct and personal relationship between a person and God, conducted based on ways instituted by God and in ways acceptable unto God, not limited to strict adherences of rituals or observances, and which is conducted in truth.

I suppose religion could be that simple. Unfortunately, religion in contemporary terms is a bit more complicated — as many practices pass for religion — in fact very complicated.

Having explored the origin and true meaning of religion, let us now briefly examine contemporary understanding and concept of religion — what is defined as and what could qualify as religion.

Religion in contemporary terms.

Below are a few definitions of religion:

> "the belief in and worship of a superhuman controlling power, especially a personal God or gods." (Oxford Encyclopaedic English Dictionary)

> "a particular system of faith and worship." (Google)

> "a set of beliefs, values, and practices based on the teachings of a spiritual leader." (Free Dictionary online)

These definitions have been purposely selected as they, severally and jointly, paint a more accurate picture of present-day understanding and concept of religion. The world today recognises virtually any and all practices as religion once such practices are presented by someone or anyone as such. And so any system of beliefs, for instance, could be constituted and widely accepted as religion. Consequently, religion though originally simple has become complex and complicated.

The overall effect is that it now is a tad difficult to rightly engage in that all-important relationship with the Creator, since there are now many ways presented as the right way to relate with God, which leaves us rather confused.

Is there a right way to relate with God? I believe there is.

And because our success in life depends largely on our relationship with our maker — God — it is pertinent that we engage in that relationship in the right and acceptable manner. Otherwise a wrong or unacceptable relationship could be very damaging, misleading, or unproductive. A relationship conducted in wrong ways wouldn't be fit for purpose — it would fail to deliver the intended results.

Before we examine that right way, let us first demonstrate the mindset element of religion based on contemporary understandings and concepts — and observe how our original religious beliefs, inclinations or leanings could easily have been influenced by our birth circumstances.

Contemporary religion as a mindset:

There is a mindset element to contemporary religion and to help demonstrate this let us consider the following few scenarios:

- A person is born somewhere in Saudi Arabia to Muslim parents, he is named Ahmed or she is named Halima; Ahmed or Halima is most likely to begin life as a Muslim believing and adhering to Islamic beliefs, teachings and practices — essentially because he or she was brought up that way.
- The same person is now born somewhere in Italy to Catholic parents, he is now called Peter or she is now called Agatha; Peter or Agatha is most likely to originally turn out a Catholic — having been brought up as one — and both might wholly believe in the beliefs, teachings and practices of Catholicism.
- The same person is now born somewhere in India to Hindu parents, he is called Anuj or she is called Akhila; Anuj or Akhila is most likely to become a Hindu — largely as a result of his or her upbringing — wholly believing in Hindu beliefs, teachings and practices.

- The same person is now born somewhere in England to Anglican parents, he is called Henry or she is called Elizabeth; Henry or Elizabeth would most likely become an Anglican — simply as result of what he or she was taught as a child — and could strongly uphold Anglican beliefs, teachings and practices.

First note how the same person has turned out differently and largely due to his or her particular birth circumstances. It means that Ahmed could easily have become Henry, Peter, or Anuj while Halima could easily have become Agatha, Akhila, or Elizabeth. In both cases, however, it is not only the names that could easily have changed but also the religious beliefs and disposition of each individual.

What this shows is that our concept of what is the right or wrong religion — religion as defined and constituted contemporarily — is originally determined by where and to whom we are born. Imagine that!

A bit disturbing when we put into consideration the fact that regional demographics of contemporary religions is largely influenced by human factors — the dominance of particular types of contemporary religions in different parts of the world is a human orchestration. More disturbing because of the significance to each person of the need to conduct his or her relationship with God in the right and acceptable manner — a condition which could greatly affect the quality of our lives.

It is possible then that your present religious beliefs are merely largely a product of a mindset — influenced by the things you have been taught as a child — and that you might've become a Muslim, Catholic, Hindu, Anglican, etc., mainly because you were brought up as one.

Mindsets are not necessarily all right and they are not necessarily all positive or productive. (We have already identified a few negative and unhealthy mindsets.) Mindsets are largely a result of the things we are exposed to. For instance, we may believe some people are a superior breed, men are more important than women, or younger people are more valuable than very old people simply because we were brought up believing so even though none of the above is true or correct. But such is how mindsets are acquired — based largely on information alone, not facts. If we are brought up believing lies we may grow up strongly upholding such lies believing them to be truths and possibly willing to die for them. Which sort of underlines the need for each of us to ensure that our religiousness is not merely a product of a mindset largely occasioned by the circumstances of our birth.

A wrong religious mindset is a big obstacle to rightly engaging in a relationship with God. Consequently, there is the need to ensure our relationship with God is not based on a mindset (possibly acquired from birth as a result of our particular upbringing). We need to at some point objectively and critically examine our religious beliefs for the purpose of determining their truthfulness and authenticity and for the purpose of securing deep personal convictions that we are doing the right things and in the right way.

Let us now see why it is not all religious practices that are right.

We shall start from when that original relationship between God, Adam and Eve was severed.

The separation from God.

Recall that Adam and Eve hid from the voice of the Lord God — when we explored the origin of religion. They hid because they had done something wrong — they had transgressed an instruction given to them by God and their disobedience resulted in a severed relationship. (Details can be found in Genesis 3:1 - 19.)

> And he said, I heard thy voice in the garden, and I was afraid, because I was naked; and I hid myself. (Genesis 3: 10; KJV)

Because of their wrong deed, Adam and Eve hid from God thereby severing the original relationship they had with God.

A separation from God, however, was not the only consequence of their disobedience because by paying heed to the devil (in the form of the serpent) they inadvertently became exposed to the knowledge of good and evil, and they also unwittingly brought themselves under the influences of both the devil and of evil.

> And the eyes of them both were opened, and they knew that they were naked; and they sewed fig leaves together, and made themselves aprons. (Genesis 3: 7; KJV)

This exposure to the knowledge of good and evil, and wilfully yielding to the influences of both the devil and evil are largely responsible for our subsequent attempts to conduct relationships with God in wrong ways — knowing wrong (evil) meant we could do wrong including doing things wrongly; also yielding to the devil meant we would subsequently become prone and vulnerable to the devil and evil influences.

The basis of false religion.

Knowledge of evil and our proneness to evil are largely responsible for false religious practices or false religions. The original constitution of our relationship with God changed with the transgression of Adam and Eve because that transgression exposed that relationship to a third party — the concept and influence of evil including the devil.

Consequently, our attempts to reconnect with God have variously been undermined by our knowledge of and vulnerability to evil. And so we tend to devise many ways — largely misguided or misdirected by the devil and our knowledge of evil — by which we might reconcile with God. Unfortunately, most of which are wrong, unacceptable and have been inspired by evil.

These wrong and misguided concepts are largely responsible for our contemporary religions.

But there is a right way.

The right way.

We already established that a relationship existed between God, Adam and Eve, and we also highlighted that that relationship was subsequently severed. The good news is that the relationship was soon restored and continued, that restoration effectively points us to the right way to reconcile our individual relationships with our maker.

To discover this right way we shall revisit the restoration of the relationship that existed between God, Adam and Eve.

The restoration:

> Unto Adam also and to his wife did the Lord God make coats of skins, and clothed them. (Genesis 3: 21; KJV)

This single verse contains more information than it seems to contain when considered only cursorily. After Adam and Eve transgressed, when next they had the voice of the Lord God they went into hiding — the separation. Now we read that God made them some clothing which is very significant because apart from demonstrating that their transgression had been pardoned — reconciliation — it also shows both of them (Adam and Eve) subsequently were reunited with God — reconnection.

It means that to properly understand that reconciliation process — the right way — we need to carefully examine how Adam and Eve were treated by God before they were reconnected with him.

The clothing of Adam and Eve by God holds the key to unravelling the right way.

How?

Recall that by the time Adam and Eve heard the voice of the Lord God they were already clothed. In Genesis 3:7 we read that Adam and Eve discovered their nakedness after eating the forbidden fruit, and that they also made themselves aprons from fig leaves. The implication here is, since they were already clothed there must've been other reasons for God having to make them further clothing.

It is possible God made clothing for Adam and Eve for the following reasons:

- As a symbol of pardon — forgiveness and reconciliation.

Adam and Eve had provided themselves with aprons made from fig leaves but God went ahead to make them coats from animal skin. Since animal skin (leather) is more durable and effective for clothing than leaves, one could reasonably infer that the provision made by Adam and Eve for their clothing was inadequate and insufficient for that purpose. As a result, it was necessary to equip them with clothing that would rightly fit the purpose. I believe by providing them with a new and more durable clothing, God was demonstrating his pardon for their transgression. (Another reasonable inference here could be that the ways we try to "cover our transgressions" — take care of them — are often inappropriate as they might be inadequate. And it also tends to show that only God can provide us with effective remedies for our transgressions since our various alternatives often fall short.)

- The use of animal skin is more than merely symbolic — it reveals further details about reconciliation.

For reconciliation to be effected there must be an atonement of the transgression which resulted in the separation — and atonement is only possible through the shedding of blood.

> For the life of the flesh is in the blood: and I have given it to you upon the altar to make an atonement for your souls: for it is the blood that maketh an atonement for the soul. (Leviticus 17: 11;KJV)

So it was necessary that blood was shed before Adam's and Eve's transgressions could be pardoned. The animal skin used must've come from animals killed as a sacrifice.

From this analysis, of the process by which Adam and Eve were reconciled to God, it seems reasonable to suggest that the basic elements of that reconciliation — and therefore the right way — are primarily as follows:

- Forgiveness.

The transgressions which necessitated our separation have to be pardoned by God before we could be reconciled and reconnected with him to continue a relationship with him. Since our transgressions are against God, it is only reasonable to opine only God can forgive us our transgressions especially since God dealt directly with Adam and Eve — during their reconciliation — and did not require the services of any intermediaries (e.g. angels).

- Atonement through a blood sacrifice.

Lives have to be given in exchange for the lives of the transgressors because the penalty for transgression is death.

> **The soul that sinneth, it shall die**. The son shall not bear the iniquity of the father, neither shall the father bear the iniquity of the son: the righteousness of the righteous shall be upon him, and the wickedness of the wicked shall be upon him. (Ezekiel 18: 20; KJV)

(Note it is the soul that "shall die" — indicating a spiritual death rather than a physical or natural one — and that death is occasioned by our disconnection from God, who effectively is the source of our spiritual nourishment. It means we could be alive bodily but dead spiritually. As a result of Adam's and Eve's transgressions, however, physical death was also pronounced on us (Genesis 3:19) as a secondary consequence. The atonement was made to prevent the death of the soul and not of the body.)

In summary, the right way is essentially one of atonement — through the shedding of blood — and forgiveness — provided by God directly to us and not through any intermediaries.

It is necessary to point out that even after the reconciliation of Adam and Eve to God, human beings would subsequently often transgress God's instructions — largely due to our knowledge of and proneness to evil . Consequently, reconciliations were achieved through atonement via blood sacrifices presented in line with the provisions instituted by God under the right way. With time, however, some people for whatever reasons would decide to conduct relationships with God in non-acceptable ways or ways which violated the right way instituted by God. It is such wilful departures from the right path that are largely responsible for the many practices which now constitute contemporary religion.

The origin of false religion.

The first recorded account of a false religious practice — non-acceptable and not in compliance with divine institutions — can be found in Genesis 4:1 – 7.

> But unto Cain and to his offering he had not respect. And Cain was very wroth, and his countenance fell. (Genesis 4: 5)

Here an offering by Cain — one of the sons of Adam and Eve — was rejected by God while that of his brother's, Abel, was accepted. By rejecting Cain's offering, God has simply demonstrated that not all attempts by humans to relate with him are acceptable by him. By extension we can reasonably infer that not all religious practices are acceptable unto God, and if they are not acceptable by God then they rightly qualify as false.

While we may not fully understand why God rejected Cain's offering what is clear is that it was rejected, with the implication that what we may regard a relationship with God might in truth be a practice which is unacceptable to him and therefore a conduct of false religion. A careful analysis of Cain's offering may reveal to us why it was not accepted, which in turn might reaffirm those key elements of the right way already highlighted — forgiveness and atonement through a blood sacrifice.

First we shall consider God's response to Cain which seems to offer his reasons for rejecting the latter's offering.

> **And the Lord said unto Cain, Why art thou wroth? And why is thy countenance fallen?**
> **If thou doest well, shall thou not be accepted? And if thou doest not well, sin lieth at the door.** And unto thee shall be his desire, and thou shalt rule over him.
> (Genesis 4: 6, 7; KJV)

One thing which is very clear is that God said Cain had not done well and as a result had sinned. Details of what Cain did wrongly is not provided but it suffices that God pointed out something wasn't right somewhere with Cain. In that case, before Cain could reconcile with God he first needed to make an atonement offering — which would require a blood sacrifice — but Cain had presented an offering of "the fruit of the ground", or plants (Genesis 4:3; KJV) which lacked the requirement of blood. Had he intended another type of offering — e.g. thanksgiving — which did not require blood he still would've been required to first make a blood sacrifice — to make atonement for his sins — before presenting his intended offering.

And so we can see how a violation of a single requirement for the right conduct of a relationship with God could render our overall relationship with him unacceptable no matter how well-meaning our worships or services might've been.

Cain's false religious conduct may be a first occurrence but it certainly is not the last. Starting with Cain, false or unacceptable religious practices have been perpetrated and perpetuated through time up to the present time. Some people even recognise other creatures (e.g. humans, animals, plants, sun, moon, starts, etc.), or concepts (e.g. love, fertility, wealth, life, death, etc.) as deities which are worshipped, or as intermediaries through whom (as they believe) they worship God.

Remember: True religion is based only on the one true God, and is a direct and personal relationship with him.

Owing to the deplorable, confused and helpless position humans unwittingly put themselves into it became necessary that God would, again, take steps which would help humanity rediscover that right way after many years of roaming around in spiritual darkness. God had to literally come down from heaven again (almost reminiscent of the earlier days when he used to descend from heaven to fellowship with Adam and Eve in the garden) in order to show us the right way.

This time God the Son — the Way — was sent down from heaven into the world to show us the right way.

The right way re-established.

The following is a summary of some key facts surrounding the right way as re-established through God the Son:

- God the Son was born through the power of the Holy Ghost and was given the name Yeshua (Hebrew), or Jesus in English. (Yeshua, also a common alternative form of the name Yehoshuah, means "salvation" in Hebrew. Yeshua corresponds to the Greek spelling Lesous, from which, through the Latin Lesus, comes the English spelling Jesus.)

   > But while he thought on these things, behold, the angel of the Lord appeared unto him in a dream, saying, Joseph, thou son of David, fear not to take unto thee Mary thy wife: **for that which is conceived in her is of the Holy Ghost. And she shall bring forth a son, and thou shalt call his name JESUS**: for he shall save his people from their sins. (Matthew 1: 20, 21; KJV)

- Jesus also was later called Christ — the English word "Christ" is derived from "Christos", which was used to translate into Greek the Hebrew "Mashiach" (also Messiah) meaning "anointed". Christos in classical Greek usage could mean covered in oil and thus a literal translation of Messiah.

Life

For unto you is born this day in the city of David a saviour, which is **Christ** the Lord." (Luke 2:11;KJV)

Pilate saith unto them, **What shall I do then with Jesus which is called Christ?** They all say unto him, Let him be crucified. (Matthew 27:22;KJV)

(The names — Jesus and Christ, especially the latter would play a significant role later.)

- Jesus expressly declared himself as the Son of God, and that himself and God the Father are one.

    He said unto them, But whom say ye that I am? And Simon Peter answered and said, **Thou art the Christ, the Son of the living God**.
    And Jesus answered and said unto him, Blessed art thou, Simon Bar-jona: for flesh and blood hath not revealed it unto thee, but my Father which is in heaven. (Matthew 16:15-17;KJV)

    I am my Father are one. (John 10:30;KJV)

- Jesus also expressly declared he came to the fulfil the "Law" and the "Prophets" — a reference to the Old Covenant — the old way which amongst other things required continuous sacrifices for the atonement of sin.

    Think not that I am come to destroy the law, or the prophets: I am not come to destroy, but to fulfil. (Matthew 5:17;KJV)

- Jesus confidently declared himself as the "Way", the "Truth", and the "Life", and that no one can come to God the Father except through him.

    Jesus saith unto him, I am the way, the truth, and the life; no man cometh unto the Father, but by me. (John 14:6;KJV)

- Jesus was crucified — as the perfect and final sacrifice for the sins of all mankind — fulfilling the requirement for atonement — a blood sacrifice — as originally ordained by God (as previously highlighted).

  But he was wounded for our transgressions, he was bruised for our iniquities: the chastisement of our peace was upon him; and with his stripes we are healed. (Isaiah 53:5;KJV)

  When the chief priests therefore and officers saw him, they cried out, saying, Crucify him, crucify him. Pilate saith unto them, Take ye him, and crucify him: for I find no fault in him. (John 19:6;KJV)

  When Jesus therefore had received the vinegar, he said, it is finished: and he bowed his head, and gave up the ghost. (John 19:30;KJV)

  Wherefore Jesus also, that he might sanctify the people with his own blood, suffered without the gate. (Hebrews 13:12;KJV)

- When Jesus was crucified the sins of mankind was atoned and pardon granted. (The only thing required to take advantage of this atonement and pardon is to simply ask for forgiveness, which also is another key feature of the right way as already discussed.)

  And he is the propitiation for our sins: and not for ours only, but also for the sins of the whole world. (I John 2:2;KJV)

  That if thou shalt confess with thy mouth the Lord Jesus, and shalt believe in thine heart that God hath raised him from the dead, thou shalt be saved. (Romans 10: 9;KJV)

- Jesus died and resurrected before ascending back into the heavens, in clear sight of those who were privileged to witness the incident, having accomplished his mission.

Life

He is not here, but is risen: remember how he spake unto you when he was yet in Galilee,
Saying, The Son of man must be delivered into the hands of sinful men, and be crucified, and the third day rise again.
(Luke 24: 6,7;KJV)

And it came to pass, while he blessed them, he was parted from them, and carried up into heaven. (Luke 24:51;KJV)

- Before Jesus ascended into the heavens he promised a "Comforter" — the Holy Ghost — who will dwell in those who would receive him, and will teach them all things. (Note that the Holy Ghost is able to and can teach us ALL things, and can lead us in truth. A very significant information as it implies we can know everything we need to know about our lives if we solicit the help of God through the Holy Ghost.)

  If ye love me, keep my commandments.
  And I will pray the Father, and he shall give you another Comforter, that he may abide with you for ever;
  Even the Spirit of truth; whom the world cannot receive, because it seeth him not, neither knoweth him: but ye know him; for he dwelleth with you, and shall be in you.
  I will not leave you comfortless: I will come to you.
  (John 14:15 -18;KJV)

  But the Comforter, which is the Holy Ghost, whom the Father will send in my name, he shall teach you all things, and bring all things to your remembrance, whatsoever I have said unto you.
  (John 14:26;KJV)

- The Holy Ghost descended upon the world on the Day of Pentecost, and ever since is readily available to whosoever will ask for it in the proper way.

> And when the day of Pentecost was fully come, they were all with one accord in one place.
> And suddenly there came a sound from heaven as of a rushing mighty wind, and it filled all the house where they were sitting.
> And there appeared unto them cloven tongues like as of fire, and it sat upon each of them.
> And they were all filled with the Holy Ghost, and began to speak with other tongues, as the Spirit gave them utterance. (Acts 2:1- 4;KJV)
>
> Then Peter said unto them, Repent, and be baptized every one of you in the name of Jesus Christ for the remission of sins, and ye shall receive the gift of the Holy Ghost. (Acts 2: 38;KJV)

These are some key information regarding the First Coming — of Jesus Christ who also is the Way.

Earlier in the chapter some key characteristics of religion (i.e. in its original and true form) were highlighted as follows:

- It is based on the one true God.
- It is instituted by God.
- It is a direct relationship between a person and God.
- It is void of rituals, formalities or protocols.
- It is based on truth and sincerity.

Now let us see how the right way re-established through Jesus Christ compares with those key characteristics of religion.

- It is based on the one true God.

The way re-established through Jesus Christ — God the Son — is based on God the Father — the one true God. Jesus and the Father are one.

- It is instituted by God.

Jesus was sent by God (John 3: 16), and God confirmed this during the baptism of Jesus Christ by John the Baptist (Matthew 3:17).

- It is a direct relationship between man and God.

Jesus clearly declared:

> Jesus saith unto him, I am the way, the truth, and the life: no man cometh unto the Father, but by me. (John 14:6;KJV)

He also said:

> I am my Father are one. (John 10:30;KJV)

Which implies that Jesus is not an intermediary but is God.

- It is void of rituals, formalities or protocols.

Jesus did not lay down any bogus rituals, formalities or religious protocols but instead simply declared:

> Come unto me, all ye that labour and are heavy laden, and I will give you rest. (Matthew 11:28;KJV)

His message of salvation was also very simple:

> Marvel not that I said unto thee, **Ye must be born again**. (John 3:7;KJV)

Jesus is effectively saying all we need to do to reconcile with God is: "Come" and "be born again". That simple!

- It is based on truth and sincerity.

Jesus said:

> And ye shall know the truth, and the truth shall make you free. (John 8:32;KJV)

He also said:

> Jesus saith unto him, I am the way, the truth, and the life: no man cometh unto the Father, but by me. (John 14:6;KJV)

And:

> God is a Spirit: and they that worship him must worship him in spirit and in truth. (John 4:24;KJV)

Jesus is the truth and he also emphasises the need for relating with God truthfully (or sincerely).

Now let us also compare how this way re-established through Jesus Christ compares with those basic elements of the right way as earlier highlighted in the chapter. We identified two basic features of the right way — the process instituted by God through which we could be reconciled with him — as:

- Forgiveness
- Atonement based on a blood sacrifice.

- Forgiveness.

Through the death of Jesus Christ the sins of mankind was pardoned — which was the main reason he laid down his life.

- Atonement.

Jesus was offered as a perfect and final sacrifice for the sins of mankind.

And so the right way as re-established through Jesus Christ is in conformity with both the main characteristics of religion (true religion) and the process of reconciliation originally instituted by God (which I have described as the right way). The true significance of this conclusion is it confirms the way re-established through Jesus Christ as the right way by which we may relate with God. A relationship we have already established is necessary as well as important for a successful life.

At this point it might be necessary to clarify that this re-establishment of the right way is more significant as a process than as a name — as a matter of fact, it wasn't given a name by Jesus Christ. This clarification is more necessitated by the fact that there are many practices, conducted under the auspices of the contemporary religion called Christianity, which are not in compliance with some basic prerequisites of the right way, or which do not conform with some of the main characteristics of true religion as previously discussed. The main issue here is that of ensuring our relationship with God is not based primarily on a name — e.g. Christianity — but instead on the right process — the right way. If we are to rely on names alone it is possible our relationship with God could be conducted in a way which is unacceptable unto God. And so it is very important I reiterate that the right and acceptable process by which we may relate with God hasn't been given any particular names by God — it is more a relationship through a process.

It is necessary we now take a good look at the contemporary religion of Christianity, especially since it is named after Jesus Christ. (Recall I earlier hinted that the names — Jesus and Christ — would become more significant later. It now is.) Christianity, as a name, is derived from the term "Christian", which in turn is derived from the name "Christ".

Origin of the term "Christian".

The term "Christian" is reported to have been in first use in Antioch — a town located in present-day Turkey — in reference to some earlier disciples of Jesus Christ — those who abided by his teachings.

> And when he had found him, he brought him unto Antioch. And it came to pass, that a whole year they assembled themselves with the church, and taught much people. **And the disciples were called Christians first in Antioch**. (Acts 11: 26;KJV)

It has been said that these earlier disciples were referred to as Christians mainly because they behaved like Christ — Jesus Christ. Christian therefore, effectively meant Christ-like. With time, however, the term "Christianity" — derived from "Christian" — would be used to describe the practice of the teachings of Jesus Christ. This reference would subsequently result in the use of the term "Christianity" to represent a branch of contemporary religion (or religious practices).

Let us now have a look at the history of the religion commonly referred to as "Christianity" contemporarily.

History of Christianity (as a contemporary religion).

Below is a summary of the history of the contemporary religion of Christianity.

- Early Christianity (circa 33 – 312 AD):

Following the crucifixion, death and resurrection of Jesus Christ, and his ascension back into the heavens the disciples congregated in local assemblies to worship and to fellowship. These earlier disciples were mostly native Hebrews (i.e. biological descendants of Abraham) but often colloquially generally referred to as Jews (although by proper definition a Jew is a practitioner of the religion of Judaism). In later times, however, Gentiles (i.e. non-Hebrews) who would become proselytes would also become part of these assemblies. (It was during one of such gatherings that the first outpouring of the Holy Ghost was experienced on Pentecost Day.)

Shortly after this Pentecost Day- experience, these disciples would come under intense persecutions which led to their dispersion to other regions of the world (notably Asia, Africa and Europe). (It was as a result of the dispersion of the earlier disciples the group in Antioch was later founded.) These persecutions would continue from then up until around 312 AD when Emperor Constantine of Rome converted to Christianity.

- Christianity under Roman Empire (circa 312 - 1054 AD):

Following the conversion of Emperor Constantine I to Christianity (c. 312 AD) the Edict of Milan was issued, officially recognising and legalising Christianity in the whole of the Roman empire. Emperor Constantine I, who then ruled western Rome, met with his counterpart, Emperor Licinius, who then ruled eastern Rome, in Milan in February 313 AD where the Edict of Milan was jointly agreed and issued. (This edict only recognised Christianity as a legalised religion in Rome but it did not make Christianity the official religion of the Roman empire.)

However, following the later defeat of Emperor Licinius by Emperor Constantine I in a battle, and the subsequent unification of western and eastern Rome under a single ruler — Emperor Constantine I — Christianity would experience a significant turning point as a result of Constantine's patronage and partisanship. For instance, in 325 AD Constantine called for the Council of Nicaea in a bid to achieve unity in Christendom.

In 391 AD, the Edict of Emperor Theodosius established Christianity as the official religion of the Roman Empire, but it was not until in c. 962 AD that Rome would become Holy Roman Empire under Emperor Otto I. Consequently, Christianity (i.e. the version officially adopted by the Roman Empire) would be propagated throughout most of the then Roman provinces and other independent sovereigns. (It is instructive to note that while the Roman Empire would propagate its own brand of Christianity, the brand of Christianity practiced by the direct disciples of Jesus Christ had already been propagated (and probably was still been propagated then) to most parts of the world. I suppose this parallel existence of Christianity in different forms is largely responsible for the Great Schism — the historic division between the Eastern and Western churches.)

- The Reformation and post-Reformation Era (circa 1483 - 1750):

Although the Great Schism gave cause to a lot of theological debates — between 1054 and 1483 — with different scholars proposing different interpretations and understandings of several elements of the teachings of Jesus Christ, it was not until October 31, 1517 — when a German Augustinian monk by the name of Martin Luther nailed his "95 Theses" to the door of the Castle Church in Wittenberg — that a significant achievement would be made regarding the transformation of Christianity.

Luther had originally only intended to protest against some of what he perceived as abusive practices under the teachings of the Catholic Church (i.e. Roman Christianity) — notably the practice of selling indulgences — and to address some of those concerns through debates. His act of deviance, and defiance was met with opposition by the Roman Catholic church, leading to the Reformation — the historic reformation of Christianity — and the formation of the Protestant Movement or churches. Other notable figures of the Reformation include Ulrich Zwingli (the leader of the Reformation in Switzerland), John Calvin (who was based in Geneva), and William Tyndale (who risked his life by secretly translating and printing the Bible in English at a time it was deemed illegal to do so).

- Pentecostal and Charismatic Movement Era (circa 1906 - Present):

Just as Early Christianity was, more or less, kick-started by the first outpouring of the Holy Ghost on Pentecost Day, a latter and second outpouring of the Holy Ghost will also birth the Pentecostal Movement which gave cause to the Pentecostal churches of today. That latter outpouring of the Holy Ghost happened during the famous Azusa Street Revival which took place in Los Angeles, California and was led by William J. Seymour.

Although Pentecostalism arose out of Protestantism it now presently commands a majority in contemporary Christianity, and can rightly be said to be the latest form of contemporary Christianity.

However, since the inception of Pentecostalism in early 20th century there have been other trends (though relatively minor) that have emerged either from or through Pentecostalism or other branches of contemporary Christianity. E.g. the so-called Deliverance Movement or ministries and the so-called Spiritualism Movement or Prayer Houses.

This brief historical review could help to explain the many divisions observable in present-day Christianity. Christianity today is a rather divided body with different denominations upholding different sets of beliefs and teachings (often based on personal interpretations and understandings). For instance, while some believe in openly confessing their sins to a priest, others believe that confession of sins must only be made privately to God. Similarly, while some believe in infant baptism, others believe that only adults (who have renounced their sins and have accepted Jesus Christ as their Lord and Saviour) should qualify for baptism. With adult baptisms however, some believe in full immersion in water, while others believe in a mere sprinkling of water on the head; and yet among those who believe in full immersion some believe immersion should only be once (in the name of the Father, Son and Holy Ghost), while others believe in three separate immersions. Likewise, while some believe in the baptism of the Holy Ghost (as promised by Jesus Christ), others don't. And there are many more areas with different interpretations from different groups or denominations.

It may also provide some explanations for certain practices conducted under the religion of Christianity but which have questionable origins. For instance, Christmas — celebrated annually on 25th December — which supposedly commemorates the birth of Jesus Christ but whose date coincides with the dates of the pagan festival Saturnalia — celebrated annually in ancient Rome between 17th and 25th December. Some popular Christmas traditions (e.g. kissing under the mistletoe, Christmas trees, and presenting gifts during Christmas) similarly have pagan connections (and possibly origins). Also Easter — celebrated annually sometime in early-Spring — which supposedly commemorates the crucifixion, death and resurrection of Jesus Christ derives its name from the pagan goddess of fertility, dawn or Spring — Eastre (also Estre, Estara, Ostara, or Ishtar) — whose annual festivals take place in Spring. It is believed some Easter traditions (e.g. "Easter eggs", "Easter bunny", "Ash Wednesday", and "Lent") have their origins in this pagan festival.

The overall implication here is that even within the contemporary religion of Christianity there could be practices which are not in compliance with divinely acceptable standards. It means then the right way is not confined by contemporary definitions — it does not necessarily have a name based on contemporary standards.

It was necessary to review the history of contemporary Christianity so as to present a better understanding of its various branches, and the different practices that constitute it. It is very important we also acquaint ourselves with the progressive transformation of Christianity from its original form — the brand of Christianity practiced by the earliest disciples of Jesus Christ — to its present form as represented by the many parts of contemporary Christianity. Consequently, we would better appreciate the truth that the right way — for engaging in a relationship with God — is more a process than a name.

The primary essence of the chapter is to highlight the importance of our need of a personal relationship with our maker and, more importantly, of our need to ensure we conduct such relationships in the right and acceptable manner, especially since there is a divinely instituted way by which that relationship ought to be conducted. That right way has now been highlighted and also extensively explored.

Recall that earlier in the chapter it was demonstrated that our religious inclinations may be largely a mindset — what we were taught to believe as a child based on our birth circumstances — with the implication that we might be strongly upholding religious beliefs which are not entirely based on truth and which might be false. It was also pointed out that the present demography of our contemporary religions — effectively the predominance of particular contemporary religions in different parts of the world — is largely down to human factors. And so we may have become exposed to a particular religion simply because it is the dominant religion in the part of the world we are born and not necessarily because it is right or based on truth. It is also possible we now uphold the beliefs of a particular religion only because it was the religion we were first exposed to.

Since there are many religions (contemporarily-speaking) and many religious practices, but only one right way (for the conduct of our relationship with God) it becomes obvious that we consequently have to make conscious efforts to ensure our relationship with God is conducted in compliance with the provisions of that right way. It means we have to put aside our partisanship and conscientiously scrutinise our relationship with God (or what we believe to be one) in order to ensure we are actually in a relationship with God.

Relationship with God is conducted in our spirits (not in our heads), it also is a vital necessity. To understand why a relationship with God is a vital necessity, and why we cannot relate with God in any other way but in our spirits, let us briefly revisit our creation.

> And the Lord God formed man of the dust of the ground, and breathed into his nostrils the breath of life; and man became a living soul. (Genesis 2:7;KJV)

We only became living souls — living beings — as soon as we received the "breath of life" from God. The sculpture made from the dust of the ground was just that — a lifeless sculpture — and it was only with the breath of life that it became alive. The breath of life represents our spirits and it came from God. Consequently, our spirit couldn't thrive well if denied a connection with its source — God. It is for the nourishment of our spirits that a relationship with God becomes an absolute necessity. And so it is our spirits which are connected with God in a relationship with him — it is by our spirits we can discover God. As the body requires daily nourishment using natural foods so also does the spirit require daily nourishment which is made available through a relationship with God. A relationship with God helps us to recharge and reinvigorate our spirits.

Our relationship with God begins with a reconciliation which in turn effects our reconnection to God. It begins with a new birth — a type of regeneration — of our spirits. This new birth revives our spirits (which have been previously dormant due to a disconnection from God) bringing them back to an active state. Once our spirits have been reactivated it becomes easier to walk with God because our spirits can then be responsive to the Holy Spirit. To live successful lives we must be led on our journeys — the journey of life — by the Holy Spirit. The Holy Spirit is able to guide us aright in all things at all times.

> Howbeit when he, the Spirit of truth, is come, he will guide you into all truth: for he shall not speak of himself; but whatsoever

> he shall hear, that shall he speak: and he will shew you things to come. (John 16:13;KJV)

It is actually our obedience to this leading by the Holy Spirit which qualifies us as children of God — or those in an acceptable relationship with God. It is also what can guarantee us good lives.

> For as many as are led by the Spirit of God, they are the sons of God. (Romans 8:14;KJV)

The only way we can truly discover God is by seeking him sincerely using our spirits. It is important to first discover God if we are to engage him in a relationship — a relationship which can only be rightly conducted in the spirit.

> God is a Spirit, and they that worship him must worship him in spirit and in truth. (John 4: 24;KJV)

Remember: It will be very difficult (and dangerous) to travel through an uncharted terrain without a reliable guide.

In the journey of life — which is a travel through unknown territories — the only reliable guide is the one who brought us into life — God.

Chapter 10

Who exactly is God?

The very first thing we should know is that there is indeed a God; the second is there is only one God. I suppose the only proof we need in this regard — that there is a God — is the mere fact of creation, including ourselves.

Now let me quickly make a few clarifications about the name "God" because, although it is presently largely used in formal reference to the Creator, in the past it has also been used to refer to other things which mostly are beyond the natural.

According to wikipedia:

> "The English word **God** continues the Old English **God (gup, gudis** in Gothic, **gud** in modern Scandinavian, **God** in Dutch, and **Gott** in modern German), which is thought to derive from Proto-Germanic **gudan**."

It has been said that the name "God" had been originally used to refer to things or concepts considered supernatural or which possess divine qualities. "God" had been used in reference to, e.g. the act of pouring libations, making invocations, saying of prayers, and in some cases for the identification of idols. It has often been used in association with things considered supernatural. It is believed that the earliest use of the word

"God" in Germanic writing is in the Gothic Bible (or Wulfila Bible, named after Wulfila, also known as Bishop Ulfillas, who translated the Bible into Gothic) in reference to the Creator. As a form of distinction a capital letter "G" is always used to precede the spelling of God in reference to the Creator while lower case "g" is used when referring to idols and other deities. My use of the word "God" therefore is strictly in reference to the Creator, and it is based on common usage. (Please note that not every modern use of the word "God" refers to the Creator as some present use of "God" — apparently in reference to a "universal deity" or "sovereign entity" — tends to recognise the existence of more than one God. When "God" is used to refer to anything that is regarded as a supernatural being, and not specifically in reference to the Creator, "God" in that sense is not a correct reference to God Almighty.)

God — our creator and maker — has been attributed with many names and references, and has also introduced himself in many different ways and by the use of equally many different names. For instance, in Exodus 6:3 (KJV) we read:

> And I appeared unto Abraham, unto Isaac, and unto Jacob, by the name of God Almighty, but by my name JEHOVAH was I not known to them.

The name Jehovah in English is derived from the Hebrew YHWH (also YHVH in older styles of writing), which could be pronounced in one of many ways depending on what vowels are used (original Hebrew writings were void of vowels). The common pronunciations of YHWH are "Yah – weh" and "Ye – ho – wah"; Jehovah is derived from the latter pronunciation.

Having dealt with the important issue of nomenclature, let us now try to understand who this God is. A very good way of establishing an understanding of who God is would be by looking at his various attributes. Before we do a more comprehensive analysis of some key attributes of God, however, let us briefly look at a few other self-introductions by God (just as the one above).

- I am Alpha and Omega, the beginning and the ending, saith the Lord, which is, and which was, and which is to come, the Almighty. (Revelation 1:8;KJV)
- I am Alpha and Omega, the beginning and the end, the first and the last. (Revelation 22:13;KJV)

God declares himself as the beginning — meaning he preceded all things; before him there was nothing — therefore everything else came into existence after God. It then means God is responsible for everything which is in existence, God is the creator of all things. God also declares himself as the ending — meaning after God there will be nothing else — effectively indicating that God is endless or never-ending.

> **And God said unto Moses, I AM THAT I AM**: and he said, Thus shalt thou say unto the children of Israel, I AM hath sent me unto you. (Exodus 3:14;KJV)

It is instructive noting that God refers to himself in the present tense — I AM — because it tends to suggest that he is in the present. Also note God did not give an elaborate description of himself but just a simple "I AM". I wonder if God did not bother to elaborate upon who he is for specific reasons. Could it be that even if he tried to it might still be difficult for Moses to comprehend? Or could it be because Moses did not have to fully know who God is? I would like to believe that it is rather impossible to fully comprehend who God is using our limited human minds. As hard as we may try we could still never fully comprehend who God is. I believe we may only be able to comprehend God in parts, depending on the parts he decides to reveal to us.

I will like to compare our limited abilities and capacities, with respect to being able to fully comprehend who God is, with that of a very young child trying to comprehend the concept of death. A very young child could never truly understand what it means to die. And so in trying to explain death to such a child, an adult might say the dead person has gone to heaven or is gone on a very long journey and may not be returning.

I also often like to compare our limited capacity (with respect to being able to fully comprehend God) to that of a single-celled organism (e.g. amoeba) trying to understand the complex workings of a multi-celled organism (e.g. humans). An organism which can only perform a single function at a time, or only the same function all through its existence would find it very difficult comprehending how it is possible to perform more than one function at the same time, many times, and all the time. Aside from seeming impossible, such abilities would also seem unrealistic to the single-celled organism.

And so it may be that God in describing himself simply as "I am" did so because Moses could still not comprehend even if he had tried to elaborate a bit more. And herein lies our single biggest problem — that of trying to comprehend God purely from a human perspective. For instance, we may wonder how it is possible for God to be omniscient — possessing knowledge of all things — or omnipresent — everywhere, same time, all the time — but only because such possibilities are alien to us. It is often by trying to comprehend God in this context — as a natural being like ourselves — that we fail in our efforts, often misunderstanding who he is and underestimating his abilities and capabilities. I would suppose our biggest error would be in assuming that God is like us. God is simply incomprehensible, at least with a human mind.

Consequently, the best way to try to comprehend God would be through our spirits, because the spirit has more capabilities than the mind. Even then we may still not be able to fully comprehend God, but at least it would yield more positive results.

It is not necessary for us to completely unravel who God is — we really do not need to know everything about God — but for us to properly relate with him it is important we know as much about him as is humanly possible. It is necessary to know the other party in a relationship if that relationship is to be conducted properly and if it is to be useful.

God is largely invisible to the human eyes, so our knowledge and understanding of him can only be possible through belief. And so let us briefly look at belief as a concept.

The concept of Belief.

We may believe something only because it is tangible and visible to us — what we may consider as facts; we may also believe without a tangible and visible representation — what we may refer to as intuition. I will like to focus more on the latter type of belief.

As humans, we are naturally endowed with the ability to believe even without seeing. We are endowed with the supernatural ability of unconscious consciousness or conviction — the ability to believe without prior conscious or deliberate reasoning.

I will try to demonstrate using a few illustrations as follows:

- A woman might conceive and almost instantly she is convinced what is growing in her womb is a human. She does not have to consciously reason before believing it is a human that is in her womb. It is arguable such convictions might be due to natural precedence — that of other pregnancies resulting in human babies — but I doubt any woman actually relies on the fact of other women's pregnancies resulting in human babies for their personal convictions that their conception is of a human baby. So, how does a woman automatically know she is pregnant with a human child?
- We generally believe other creatures (e.g. plants, oceans, or animals) are not able to directly communicate with us (as humans) either verbally or non-verbally (but especially verbally, for creatures that are capable of vocal expression). We simply know we couldn't have a proper conversation with non-humans even without first personally trying. Is it possible though that other creatures may actually be able to hear us speak, for instance? We have no definite proof, yet we are convinced that they cannot. Why?

- We wake up each morning and we get out of bed placing our feet on the floor without first checking if the floor will hold or give way; we simply know the floor will hold.
- We hurry to the bathroom and turn the tap on without first thinking whether water will flow from it or not; we just know water will gush out from the tap as soon as we turn it on.
- We get dressed, walk to the car and we turn the car keys without first thinking if the car will start or not; we just know that once we turn on the ignition the car will come to life.
- We arrive at work confident of meeting a building with all the infrastructures that make up our workplaces in place, without first confirming if the building had somehow vanished overnight, burnt down or had been blown away by the wind; we just know that we will meet our workplaces just as we left them the last time.
- We make our ways to appointments very confident of meeting the other party without first deciding whether or not to trust that such parties would honour the appointments as scheduled; we simply know that when we get to the venues we will meet with the other party.
- We work all week or month expecting a salary at the end without first convincing ourselves whether we will actually be paid or not; we simply naturally know that we will be adequately remunerated for the work done at the end of each interval as contracted.
- We book a holiday to places we have never been before (but probably only heard or read about) without first confirming that such places actually exist; we just know such places are not mere imaginary or fictitious locations.
- At the end of each work day we confidently make our ways to our respective homes very certain that our homes are still where we left them, without first thinking whether our homes are still where we left them or if something might've happened to them in our absence; we just know that we will find our homes just as we had left them.

Why and how are we able to exercise such confidences, convictions or beliefs? I reason that we are able to do all of these only because we have been endowed with the natural ability to unconsciously belief without prior reasoning or deliberation. In my opinion, it is this belief — which transcends natural reasoning and consciousness, which often is referred to as intuition — that makes a person aware and certain of the existence of God even without first directly encountering him on a personal level, in a specific or profound way. We simply know deep down in our spirits that there is a God.

We often refer to the Holy Bible as "the word of God", because its contents are divinely inspired and relate primarily to God. And so in trying to understand who God is, it is also necessary we take a brief look at the book which is called the Holy Bible and none the least because its contents provide the basis of most of our convictions.

The Holy Bible.

You would've already realised that from the beginning of the book I have used the Bible as a primary source for most of the references I make, and in a manner which suggests that I believe it to be an authority and its contents authentic and irrefutable. Yes I do. I do not only believe in the Bible because it has been presented as a holy book, but because of my personal conviction about the authenticity of its contents as products of divine inspiration. I believe it contains divine truths and I believe God still speaks through its contents.

However, I am not unaware that some contents of the Bible have somehow been exposed to a few human influences, some of which might've been deliberate and others which might have been inadvertent. For instance, I am not unaware that in compiling some versions of the Bible some elements of the original Scriptures from which it was complied were either deliberately omitted or somewhat abridged. For instance, I am aware of the Apocrypha which apparently is a collection of books, scripts, or accounts not included in the official version of the Bible. I am also aware some of the existing books in some versions of the Bible are missing some chapters or verses available in their original source. Similarly, I am not unaware that while translating the contents of the Bible from its original languages to some primary languages, and subsequently to other latter modern languages, some meanings have been either deliberately or inadvertently misrepresented or wrongly translated so that their original meanings and contexts have become distorted or somehow lost during such translations.

These human influences, however, cannot and do not undermine the authenticity of the contents of the Bible — its contents are still genuine nonetheless. Some books may have been omitted but that does not affect the authenticity of the things that have been included. More over, I believe that even those things that have been omitted, where they become necessary for a person to become aware of them, can be brought to the awareness of such persons by God, through the Holy Spirit, as and when required. (Personally, I have experienced this as I have been led on a few occasions to some elements of the Apocrypha.) Some words, phrases, or sentences may have been wrongly translated but I believe that the Holy Spirit can and does provide sincere seekers with the right and original meanings of those things which have been mistranslated, and not only their original meanings but other meanings that might specifically apply to each person and under different circumstances. (Which is why I said God still speaks through the contents of the Bible.)

In conclusion, I wholly believe in the authenticity, divinity and authority of the Bible.

In forging a relationship with God, however, we are not to be limited to the contents of the Bible because God is in the present and he still speaks (even as he spoke in times past). And so although the Bible should be a key element in our relationship with God, our relationship with him should not be restricted to the contents of the Bible alone because God can speak to us in many other ways even as he speaks through the contents of the Bible.

Having looked at belief, as a concept, and having also dealt with the issue of the Bible (as an authority and its contents authentic) we shall now begin to explore a few attributes of God.

One God; Three persons.

There is only one God. There are not many gods, and also there are not different gods or forms of gods.

> **I am the Lord, and there is none else, there is no God beside me**: I girded thee, though thou hast not known me: (Isaiah 45:5;KJV)

God, however, exists in three distinct and different personalities — the Father, the Son and the Holy Ghost, but all of whom are one and same person. The first hint of this multiple personality of God's can be found at the very beginning of creation in Genesis 1:26(KJV):

> **And God said, Let us make man in our image, after our likeness**: and let them have dominion over the fish of the sea, and over the fowl of the air, and over the cattle, and over all the earth, and over every creeping thing that creepeth upon the earth.

"Us" and "our" in the above quotation denotes a plurality, which I believe refers to the multiple-personality of God. And then, Jesus Christ made a statement in John 17:21 (KJV) which also clearly denotes a multiple-personality:

> That they all may be one; **as thou, Father, art in me, and I in thee**, that they also may be one in us: that the world may believe that thou hast sent me.

The above tends to provide more insight into the composition of this multiple-personality a Father and Jesus (whom we know as the Son).

And in Genesis 1:2 (KJV):

> And the earth was without form, and void; and darkness was upon the face of the deep. **And the Spirit of God moved upon the face of the waters**.

Here we are introduced to the Spirit of God who, in addition to the Father and Son, make up this multiple-personality of God's commonly referred to as the triune God — the three all of whom were revealed in their various distinct forms during the baptism of Jesus Christ as recorded in Matthew 3:16, 17 (KJV):

> And **Jesus**, when he was baptized, went up straightway out of the water: and, lo, the heavens were opened unto him, and he saw the **Spirit of God** descending like a dove, and lighting upon him:

> And lo **a voice from heaven**, saying, This is my **beloved Son**, in whom I am well pleased.

And so the multiple-personality of God comprises only of the Father, Son and Holy Ghost, but whom all exist as one. It may appear slightly confusing trying to comprehend this multiple-personality nature of God's and so I will attempt to help here by pointing out that human beings, as a matter of fact, also have a multiple personality, howbeit one of a more limited nature. Each person is made up of a natural and spiritual component — a body and also a spirit, both of which are separate, distinct and function as a single entity one person. It is not possible to see a spirit and so when we look at a person what we often only see is the body. But a body could not exist without a spirit — except a lifeless body — meaning that although what we often see is a body, that body actually exists as part of a multiple-personality in a single entity and has another integral component — the spirit which ordinarily is invisible to the human eyes. There have been a few instances where some people have experienced what is often referred to as an out-of-body experience (probably because they were in a coma, in an unconscious state or momentarily clinically-dead); some of such people have claimed to have observed themselves "stepping out" from their bodies while still able to see their bodies where they were laid. I suppose it was the spirits of such people that "stepped out" from their physical bodies in such circumstances when their spirits were momentarily separated from their bodies. This simply helps to demonstrate the nature and possibility of multiple-personality existence.

As humans, we have a distinct body which is different from an equally distinct spirit but both of which exist as a single individual. Similarly, there is only one God, but who exists in a multiple-personality as — Father, Son and Spirit.

God is omnipotent.

God is all-powerful and he possesses a complete and unlimited power hence he is also referred to as the Almighty or God Almighty.

> God hath spoken once; twice have I heard this; that power belonged unto God. (Psalms 62:11:KJV)

It is instructive to note that power, in its entirety, belongs to God because some people often wrongly presume power is divisible and exists in parts such that while some powers ("good power") are under the control of God, a few other powers ("evil power") are controlled by other forces (mainly evil and the devil). (I was one of such people — who wrongly presumed that God was in control of some powers while the devil controlled a few — until I became properly enlightened through the aid of the Holy Spirit.) Power is absolute and does not exist as good and evil, rather it is how power is applied that could make it seem good or evil. And it belongs to God — power is under God's authority.

In discussing power, it is very important to also point out that, contrary to what some people might believe, there is no power outside the direct authority of God; there can be no exercising of power without God permitting such. Some people presume the devil has got his own range of evil powers which he can wield at will. The truth, however, is that the only power the devil (or any other spirits) can exercise are those allowed them by God. God has endowed most of his creation with different abilities and capabilities, meaning that we can exercise those abilities at will without God necessarily having to interfere with our choices. God may permit our choices (including how we choose to apply the powers we are naturally endowed with) even where such choices contradict his will. But this does not imply that such exercising of powers is beyond God's control.

Generally-speaking, things are only made possible either because God had orchestrated them (in which case God is directly responsible for them), or because he had permitted them to happen, even where they are not his original designs or wishes (in which case others are directly responsible for them) —— but both are still under God's authority and none could happen if he does not allow their occurrence.

The devil and other evil spirits are also bound by this principle — they couldn't exercise any powers without God's permission. Like human beings, the devil has some abilities and capabilities he is already endowed with (as a result of his former status as an angel), but which, I suppose, have been somewhat limited (as a result of his disobedience, since some of our natural endowment of abilities are conditional and subject to our satisfying our part of the agreement), and which he can freely exercise (again limited to the original constitution of such powers because our endowments, including power, can only be automatic when applied as originally established or ordained) but ultimately subject to God's authority. In other words, if God decides to overrule a particular use of power then even where such powers are exercised they would not be effective in achieving their intended results.

To help demonstrate that the devil could not exercise powers arbitrarily without God's authority we shall use the story of Job as a model. (Details can be found in Job 1 - 42)

The story has it that on a certain day, when the sons of God came to present themselves before the Lord, Satan also came among them. A conversation ensued between God and Satan during which God remarked about Job's faithfulness and integrity, but Satan responded as follows:

> Hast not thou made an hedge about him, and about his house, and about all that he hath on every side? Thou hast blessed the work of his hands, and his substance is increased in the land. (Job 1:10;KJV)

The devil's response seems to suggest that he was incapable of afflicting Job, had he wanted to, because of the "hedge" placed around Job by God.

If the devil could not afflict Job it is possibly only because he just was not able to — he lacked the ability to; he was powerless. The devil then went ahead to challenge God to "put forth thine hand now, and touch all that he hath" — in other words to afflict Job — to which God responded as follows:

> And the Lord said unto Satan, Behold, all that he hath is in thy power; only upon himself put not forth thine hand. So Satan went forth from the presence of the Lord. (Job 1:12;KJV)

It was only after this authorisation of the devil by God that the former was able to afflict Job, he could not have done anything had God not empowered him — and even at that the devil could do only as much as he was allowed to; the devil could only destroy Job's possessions ("all that he hath") but he could not physically afflict Job ("only upon himself put not forth thine hand"), just as he was permitted and enabled. I believe the devil did not physically afflict Job not out of obedience to God but only because he simply did not have the power to do so.

As the story progresses, the devil was permitted by God to afflict Job physically but not to take his life; again, the devil was only able to do as empowered but he could not kill Job. I suppose, only because he simply could not — he wasn't given the power to.

This story clearly demonstrates that power belongs to God, and that only when God empowers somebody can such a person exercise the powers given to him or her. It also shows that the devil does not have his own powers or powers that are outside the authority of God. Sadly, sometimes we unwittingly yield our abilities to the devil thereby making certain things possible and oftentimes when such things happen we wrongly attribute them to the devil or to his abilities. As a result we wrongly believe that the devil has more powers than he has been given.

God is all-powerful and nothing is impossible for him.

> For with God nothing shall be impossible. (Luke 1:37;KJV)

God is Omniscient.

God is all-knowing and there is nothing beyond his knowledge or understanding. God knows the past, present and future and he knows the end even before its beginning.

> Hast thou not known? hast thou not heard, that the everlasting God, the Lord, the Creator of the ends of the earth, fainteth not, neither is weary? **there is no searching of his understanding**. (Isaiah 40:28;KJV)

> Remember the former things of old: for I am God, and there is none else; I am God, and there is none like me, Declaring the end from the beginning, and from ancient times the things that are not yet done, saying, My counsel shall stand, and I will do all my pleasure: (Isaiah 46:9,10;KJV)

Only God has knowledge of all things, as there is none other who has this ability. Some people also wrongly presume the devil knows almost everything; they believe the devil can read their minds, is privy to their every thoughts and can correctly predict the future. (I also was previously under this wrong impression, until God enlightened me with the truth.) The truth is that the devil is not only limited with respect to power but also in many other aspects including knowledge; the devil possesses limited knowledge, he doesn't know every of God's plans (either for us personally or for the world in general), he doesn't know every of our thoughts, and he doesn't know everything about the future (e.g. he doesn't know when the world would be brought to an end). I suppose the knowledge the devil possesses is largely based on those things he was already privy to as a result of his former status and also whatever new information he is able to garner, subsequent to his fall, from any available sources (e.g. humans, who may unwittingly make revelations verbally in the presence of unseen evil spirits, and also other evil spirits who are in association with the devil).

Again, using the story of Job as a reference a few deductions could be made which helps to demonstrate that devil's knowledge is limited. For instance, had the devil been able to predict the future he probably would've known that Job was never going to falter or become unfaithful to God no matter how bad he was afflicted. And so he wouldn't have bothered trying in the first place.

A different example is that of the crucifixion of Jesus Christ. I suppose the devil would've been aware of Jesus' mission on earth but what he might not have known was how that mission was to be accomplished. I would imagine that had the devil known Jesus' mission would be accomplished by his death he wouldn't have tried very hard to influence his death by manipulating the people involved in his death. I suppose the devil sought to prevent Jesus from fulfilling his mission hence the many attempts to kill him prematurely, starting from when he was born (the many children killed as a result of the decree from King Herod in an attempt to kill the infant Jesus) even though none of those attempts proved successful. What the devil didn't know, however, was that Jesus actually came to lay down his life for all of mankind — he came to die. I believe this also helps to demonstrate the limited nature of the knowledge which the devil possesses.

God (and him alone) knows everything, including everything you may need to know about your existence in particular and life in general.

God is Omnipresent.

God is continuously and simultaneously present everywhere and all the time.

> Am I a God at hand, saith the Lord, and not a God afar off? Can any hide himself in secret places that I shall not see him? saith the Lord. **Do not I fill heaven and earth?** saith the Lord. (Jeremiah 23:23,24;KJV)

Again, only God can be everywhere, same time, all the time. Some people wrongly believe the devil has the ability to be at more than one place at the same time, but he simply cannot. To better understand what the capabilities of the devil are it might be necessary pointing out that he is simply a spirit a fallen angel. Spirits are able to move about relatively quicker than physical bodies but they cannot be at more than one place at the same time — to be at any particular place spirits have to first get there. The devil and all the other evil spirits have to transport themselves from places to places in order to be at such places but they are not and cannot be everywhere all the time. Sadly, limited by space and numbers, evil spirits often rely on humans to assist them establish presence in places that they are not momentarily present, although sometimes the humans involved may be completely unaware they are been used for such purposes. For instance, the devil may seek to torment a particular person and may influence someone, who is usually around the intended victim, to do some harmful things to him or her (either physically or emotionally) even when the devil or other evil spirits are not anywhere near such victims at the time or times of his or her afflictions in the hands of a fellow human being. It means that the devil does not have to be present with the intended victim before he or she could be tormented by the devil. And so a person, operating under the influence of the devil and having already been filled with murderous desires, might later embark on a killing spree, for instance, whereas the devil was no where around the location of his or her killings at the time such killings took place.

Based on the foregoing exposé, it would seem that the devil seeks to manipulate us into believing he is more than he really is, and able to do more than he really can — e.g. that he has more powers and knows more than he actually does, and that he is everywhere whereas he is not and cannot — probably so he can utilise such false notions and the associated ignorance to his advantage and to our detriment because wrongly believing that your opponent in a fight is able to do more than he or she can actually do can be very intimidating, counterproductive, demoralising and could leave us defeatist. The good news, however, is that the devil is not what he pretends he is; the better news is that now we know.

Another good news is that since God is omnipresent, he is with us all the time and the implication of that is that God is nearer to us than the devil is, and all the time.

God is infallible.

God cannot make mistakes, cannot be wrong, and cannot fail simply because he just cannot. It might be a bit difficult trying to understand infallibility using a human mind but when we put into consideration that God is omniscient, omnipresent and omnipotent then his infallibility becomes rather obvious and a bit more easier to comprehend.

History tends to validate the infallibility of God because many historical accounts reveal God as infallible. For instance, it is obvious that God didn't make a mistake by giving us the freedom of choice — which meant we could go contrary to God's wishes and expectations — because in the end that gesture only goes to prove to us how much he loves us; God loves us so much he didn't want to confine or limit us in any ways. We are given the freedom of choice on purpose and for good reasons.

Similarly, it was not wrong that God brought the first world (in the days of Noah) to an end because of their disobedience — because they were warned repeatedly about the consequences of their actions and even about the impending flood; moreover, they were also provided with a way of escape (Noah's ark) meaning that those who wanted could've avoided the inevitable destruction that befell most. Besides, the destruction of the old world also serves as a good reminder and a warning to the people that subsequently would repopulate the earth (us) that God keeps to his decrees — that too also serves a purpose.

Everything God does — even those things which might not seem to make sense to us and so may be regarded as mistakes or failures — are for a purpose.

God is infallible; it means we can completely trust him in all things.

God cannot lie.

God cannot lie — for the simple reason that he cannot — because whatever he says is — it comes into effect. Whatever God says comes to be. For instance, in the beginning when darkness pervaded the earth; God said, Let there be light: and there was light. (Genesis 1:3; KJV)

God's word is life itself, it creates and it is self-fulfilling, which is why he expressly declares accordingly:

> So shall my word be that goeth forth out of my mouth: it shall not return unto me void, but it shall accomplish that which I please, and it shall prosper in the thing whereto I sent it. (Isaiah 55:11;KJV)

Therefore, if everything God says comes to be then he just couldn't lie.

To help demonstrate the immutability of whatever God says, I will like to use the story of King Ahab and his wife, Queen Jezebel. (Details can be found in I Kings 21 and 22; and II Kings 9.)

The story goes as follows: King Ahab, the king of Samaria, wanted a particular vineyard which belonged to one of his subjects called Naboth. Having been refused the piece of land, after having offered to pay for it or to give another piece of land in exchange, he was displeased and became miserable. His wife, Queen Jezebel, found the king in this sad state and, having been made aware of the reason for his misery, chided him for his petulance while also assuring him that she will eventually make the vineyard his. She then hatched an evil plan — which included framing Naboth and wrongfully convicting him of blasphemy against God — as a result of which Naboth was taken outside the city and stoned to death. With Naboth dead it became easy for Ahab to usurp his vineyard, just as Jezebel had promised.

Now the real drama begins.

As soon as this happened God instructed prophet Elijah:

> And **the word of the Lord** came to Elijah the Tishbite, saying, Arise, go down to meet Ahab king of Israel, which is Samaria:

> behold, he is in the vineyard of Naboth, whither he is gone down to possess it.
> And thou shalt speak unto him, saying, Thus saith the Lord, Hast thou killed, and also taken possession? And thou shalt speak unto him, saying, **Thus saith the Lord, In the place where dogs licked the blood of Naboth shall dogs lick thy blood, even thine.** (I Kings 21:17 - 19;KJV)

And also:

> And of Jezebel also **spake the Lord, saying, The dogs shall eat Jezebel by the wall of Jezreel.** (I Kings 21:23;KJV)

After these incidents Ahab reigned in relative peace, and there were no wars between Israel (Samaria) and her neighbours (particularly Syria). After about three years, however, during a visit from the king of Judah, Ahab decided it was time to recapture one of his cities — Ramoth, Gilead — which had fallen into the hands of the king of Syria. A war was therefore declared between Israel and Syria and for this purpose Ahab enlisted the support of King Jehoshaphat, the visiting king of Judah. Before proceeding to the battle, Ahab attempted some form of disguise so as to appear incognito — he decided not to wear his royal battle robes — while encouraging Jehoshaphat to go into battle fully clad in his royal battle robes. Ahab's attempt at disguise was for good reason — I suppose to deflect attention from himself, rightly expecting to be a primary target — because for this battle the king of Syria commanded his army:

> But the king of Syria commanded his thirty and two captains that had rule over his chariots, saying, Fight neither with small nor great, save only with the king of Israel. (I Kings 22:31;KJV)

Ahab's ingenious plans almost succeeded because Jehoshaphat would soon become the primary target of the Syrian soldiers, but he cried out and his pursuers, realising that he wasn't the particular king they were after, turned back from pursuing him. And then this happens:

> And a certain man drew a bow at a venture, and smote the king of Israel between the joints of the harness: wherefore he said unto the driver of his chariot, Turn thine hand, and carry me out of the host; for I am wounded.
> And the battle increased that day: and the king was stayed up in his chariot against the Syrians, **and died at even: and the blood ran out of the wound into the midst of the chariot**. (I Kings 22:34,35;KJV)

And the battle is over!

But the story is not, and continues. However, we will now pause so as to reflect on what has happened so far. I wonder what prompted Ahab to declare war against Syria at this particular time — not before and not later — and also why he felt it necessary then to recapture a city that had since been in the enemy's hands for a reasonable length of time. Now also consider the following:

- Ahab, rightly suspecting he would be highly sought after, went into battle disguised.
- The king of Syria commands his captains to spare every other enemy but Ahab.
- Jehoshaphat, dressed in royal battle robes, almost got killed because the Syrian soldiers presumed he was Ahab.
- A Syrian soldier makes a random aim, not particularly at Ahab, but incidentally hits Ahab, and exactly where he was exposed and vulnerable thereby killing him.

Is it possible these all happened merely by chance?

To conclude this part of the story, let us see what happened after Ahab died in battle.

> And one washed the chariot in the pool of Samaria; and the dogs licked up his (Ahab's) blood; and they washed his armour;

according unto the word of the Lord which he spake. (I Kings 22:38;KJV)

So Ahab sustains mortal injuries in a battle, he bleeds to death in his chariot, is taken home and buried while the chariot is taken to the pool and cleaned and in the process his blood was licked by dogs, just as God had said through prophet Elijah. It is instructive noting that had Ahab not died in a battle he probably wouldn't have died bleeding (especially not in his chariot); had he not bled in his chariot his blood would probably not have found its way somewhere dogs could have access to it; and finally, that for it to happen exactly as God had said, Ahab had to have died the very way he did. Chance? Probably not. (Maybe this was why Ahab was prompted to desire recapturing Ramoth in the first place and at the time that he did, which was why he declared war against Syria; it seems he needed to be killed at war for God's word to be fulfilled exactly as spoken.)

Now for the second and concluding part of the story — Jezebel's ordeal.

King Ahab was succeeded by his son, Ahaziah — who died without having a male child — and was succeeded by Jehoram — his brother, another of Ahab's sons — who became king of Samaria; and subsequently, Elijah was translated (into heaven) and was succeeded by prophet Elisha. After a very long time, Elisha instructed one of the children of the prophets to go and anoint a person named Jehu as king over Samaria in place of the reigning king, King Jehoram, effectively bringing an end to the reign of Ahab's lineage in Samaria. (Again I wonder why it was only at this particular time that an instruction originally given to Elijah many years before would be finally implemented, not even by him but by his successor.) Following his anointing as king, however, Jehu would conspire and revolt against the reigning king, King Jehoram (or Joram for short), who incidentally at the time had recently returned to Jezreel to recuperate from injuries sustained in a battle against Syria. (Does Jezreel ring a bell? It should because that was the exact place God said Jezebel's body would be eaten by dogs.)

Jehoram was eventually killed by Jehu — the former had ridden in a chariot, in the company of the king of Judah (also named Ahaziah), to meet with Jehu as he approached the fortress at Jezreel in company of his own supporters but had turned back and fled upon realising Jehu's true mission (to kill the current king, him) — after which Jehu returned to Jezreel.

The saga now continues:

> And when Jehu was come to Jezreel, Jezebel heard of it; and she painted her face, and tired her head, and looked out at a window. And as Jehu entered in at the gate, she said, Had Zimri peace, who slew his master?
> And he lifted up his face to the window, and said, Who is on my side? Who? And there looked out to him two or three eunuchs. And he said, Throw her down. **So they threw her down: and some of her blood was sprinkled on the wall, and on the horses: and he trode her under foot**.
> And when he was come in, he did eat and drink, and said, Go, see now this cursed woman, and bury her: for she is a king's daughter.
> And they went to bury her: **but they found no more of her than the skull, and the feet, and the palms of her hands**.
> Wherefore they came again, and told him. And said, **This is the word of the Lord, which he spake by his servant Elijah the Tishbite, saying, in the portion of Jezreel shall dogs eat the flesh of Jezebel**:
> And the carcase of Jezebel shall be as dung upon the face of the field in the portion of Jezreel; so that they shall not say, This is Jezebel.
> (II Kings 9:30 – 37;KJV)

End of story.

Is it possible that Jezebel's death and the manner of its occurrence happened by chance? Well it happened just as God had said it would, confirming that whatever God says happens as said. This story is a very intriguing one and it helps to demonstrate the immutability of whatever God says — it happens just as said. (I would imagine that Jezebel might've after a very long time began to presume that the prophetic pronouncement against her would never come to fulfilment, at least not in the manner it was proclaimed — with her corpse been eaten by dogs. We now know that prophecy was fulfilled and to every minute detail.)

While reflecting upon certain aspects of this story — e.g. why Ahab decided to go to war at the time he did and why it took so long before Jezebel would eventually be killed I was made aware of the timing element of everything God say — when God decrees a thing that thing, in addition to being self-fulfilling, also has a timing element to it (when it is decreed to happen). I was then made to realise that it is only when the appointed time eventually matures that events would begin to unfold which would enable the fulfilment. Such events are often divinely orchestrated so that they may occur through the actions of human beings but who may not really know why they are doing what they are doing. For instance, in the case of Ahab, he suddenly desired to recapture Ramoth, which had been captured by Syria many years before, but he may not know why he wanted to do so and at this particular time as well. Likewise, Elisha suddenly realised that Jehu had to be anointed king that particular time, but for no apparent reason even though the instruction was given several years earlier and to his predecessor even.

And so I was made to understand that once it is time, the power of God in his word — through the activities of the Holy Spirit — causes whatever is required for the performance of that word to begin to happen because every word spoken by God is self-fulfilling and also has a timing. The timing, as it were, triggers the fulfilment.

God honours his words (or decrees).

When God ordains or decrees a thing he allows it to run its full course as ordained or decreed, but he does not arbitrarily interfere with that thing just because he could (if he wanted), or because it is been implemented contrary to his intentions or even for any other reasons. God Almighty is honourable and so respects his decrees allowing them to run their courses with no interferences (except where absolutely necessary), and he always operates by the rules (even though the rules were set by him).

At creation God ordained certain things, empowering each with the ability of self-fulfilment including running their full courses. A few are mentioned below:

> And God said, Let there be lights in the firmament of the heavens to divide the day from the night; and let them be for signs, and for seasons, and for days, and years: And let them be for lights in the firmament of the heaven to give light upon the earth: and it was so. (Genesis 1:14,15;KJV)

And therefore we have daytime, night-time, days, seasons and years. You will also observe that since their decree — at creation — they have continued to operate accordingly. For instance, night always precedes day which in turn is always followed by night in an ordered continuous cycle. Similarly, with the different seasons, Winter is always before Spring, which is always before Summer, which is always before Autumn and which always precedes Winter in a similarly ordered continuous cycle. The same applies to every other aspect of creation — they obey the laws of their respective orders as ordained by the Creator. This order is always maintained simply because God ordained it so — God doesn't have to constantly monitor their performance because he has already empowered them to self-perform. In the same way, we also have been brought into existence by reason of divine decrees and we are empowered to run our full courses including the fulfilment of our respective purposes (subject only to how we exercise our freedom of choice because God would often permit our choices, except in cases where it is absolutely necessary that he intervenes, and it is possible that our choices may at times go contrary to the things he has ordained for us or ordained us for).

It might be worthwhile pointing out that God handed over to mankind almost everything he has created, giving us dominion over them (see Genesis 1:26). Consequently, God has left it to us to take care of his creation and because he has already empowered us accordingly he doesn't always interfere with us in how we handle the rest of creation. For instance, we may decide to dredge oceans, hew down forests, landfill lakes or rivers, decimate the population of particular animals, or engage in similar activities that could jeopardise the sustainability of our world thereby rendering our existence vulnerable and God would not interfere with our actions but only because he has already committed these things to our care and because he has also allowed us freedom of choice he doesn't always interfere with our choices. (It means then that we might be largely responsible for some of the things for which we often blame God. E.g. earthquakes, floods, storms, etc.)

It might also be worthwhile pointing out that, out of every creation humans are possibly to only group that seem to operate contrary to what and how they are ordained because it seems that in several ways we do violate some of the decrees which brought us into existence. (I suppose this might be because God has made us with the freedom of choice meaning that we may choose to operate contrary to his decrees.)

Below are a few points which could help to further demonstrate this particular attribute of God's:

- Humans are empowered with freewill and consequently, God does not always interfere with our choices (not even when we go contrary to his wishes).
- We are not always punished instantly whenever we disobey God's instructions because God has set a particular time during which each person would account for his or her life — what was done and what wasn't done.
- God does not destroy a life only because the person involved operates contrary to his decree for that particular person, but instead he allows each life to run its full course as originally decreed by him.
- God will not withdraw the skills, talents, and various abilities he has endowed each of us with only because they are been utilised for wrong purposes, but will allow us to utilise them as we please.

Many other instances abound but these will do. It might also be worthwhile pointing out that it is because God honours his decrees that he has allowed the devil and other erring spirits to continue to exist in disobedience, making it possible for them to continue perpetrating evil. The devil and all the other rebel spirits are allowed to run their respective courses in full, based on their respective decreeing by God, because God honours his decrees.

Another very significant aspect of this attribute of God's is to do with the timing of his decrees. I pointed out in the last section that there is a timing element to everything God says or decrees, and now I will like to also point out that God equally honours the timing he has assigned to his decrees — he wouldn't simply alter the timing of a thing arbitrarily but will allow it to be fulfilled in its time as ordained.

> To every thing there is a season, and a time to every purpose under the heaven: (Ecclesiastes 3:1;KJV)

For most things that God has decreed there are specific timings for the occurrence of each, the only exceptions being those things which God has left to our respective choices. There are certain things for which we have already been empowered to deal with as we choose — these we can influence their timings — but there are many others which are beyond our sphere of influence — and which can only happen based on God's timings for them. The focus here is on the latter. (By divine guidance I believe we would be able to distinguish between the two — the things whose timings are under our influence and those whose timings are not — as applicable in our personal lives.) Once a thing has been decreed by God it cannot happen before its timing and to help demonstrate I will refer to a few examples.

The first is with respect to the birth of Isaac to Abraham and Sarah. (Details can be found in Genesis 12 – 21) When Abraham was 75 years old God made him a promise concerning his posterity even though at the time Abraham was childless:

> And the Lord appeared unto Abram, and said, **Unto thy seed will I give this land**: and there built he an altar unto the Lord, who appeared unto him. (Genesis 12:7;KJV)

Try as he may, however, Abraham could still not conceive a child with Sarah his wife so that even though he received other assurances from God (see Genesis 13:16;15:5) he was understandably worried (see Genesis 15:2). About nine years later, when Abraham was 86 years old, a son was born to him by Sarah's maid as a result of a plan hatched by Sarah but with time God still reiterated to Abraham that Sarah would have a son for him who was to be called Isaac (see Genesis 17:19). Eventually, God's promise to Abraham was fulfilled as Sarah conceived and had a son just as God had said:

> And the Lord visited Sarah as he had said, **and the Lord did unto Sarah as he had spoken**.
> For Sarah conceived, and bare Abraham a son in his old age, **at the set time of which God had spoken to him**.
> And Abraham called the name of his son that was born unto him, whom Sarah bare to him, **Isaac**.
> (Genesis 21:1- 3;KJV)

Note carefully the phrase — "at the set time of which God had spoken to him" — which tends to imply that the promise of a child given to Abraham by God had a definite timing assigned to it. And so it wasn't a promise that could be fulfilled just at any time — it was decreed for a given time and could only be fulfilled at that time. To backup this timing aspect of the promise:

> Is any thing too hard for the Lord? At the time appointed I will return unto thee, according to the time of life, and Sarah shall have a son. (Genesis 18: 14;KJV)

The reference above makes it very clear that there is a time appointed for that particular promise. The main significance of this illustration is that it helps to demonstrate that God always honours his decrees allowing them to pan out as originally ordained, because even though while waiting for the fulfilment of the promise Abraham was at times in distress, worrisome and often fussed about his childlessness God did not still interfere with the timing of the promise but instead allowed it to run its ordained full course so that it was only fulfilled at the appointed time. Note that Abraham couldn't in any way influence or persuade God to alter the timing for the birth of Isaac, and not because God was insensitive to his plights but because God is bound by his decrees — God's words have already been empowered for self-fulfilment (and where applicable, with specific timings), and he allows them to perform as empowered. Simply because that is God's nature.

The other example is with respect to Joseph — who happens to be Abraham's great grandson. (Details can be found in Genesis 37- 46) God revealed to a young Joseph through dreams that the latter would someday reign or have authority over his siblings, and even his parents. Joseph shared his dreams with his siblings (most of whom were older than himself) and with his father, which made his siblings envious. Consequently, his brothers plotted to kill him but eventually he was sold into slavery and subsequently brought to Egypt. Joseph prospered in the house of his Egyptian master, Potiphar, but was later falsely accused, wrongly convicted and subsequently imprisoned. He would later spend many years in prison.

Eventually, Pharaoh's chief butler and chief baker were also imprisoned and it happened that both were assigned to Joseph to look after. These two royal servants subsequently had different dreams on a given night, which Joseph helped to correctly interpret — the chief baker was executed while the chief butler was restored to his former office. Before his release from prison, Joseph had implored the assistance of the chief Butler who upon regaining his freedom apparently forgot about Joseph.

Well two years later, Pharaoh also had a dream which greatly troubled him and for which he desperately needed an interpretation. Incidentally, his magicians and wise men weren't able to successfully interpret Pharaoh's dream and it was only during this time that the chief butler remembered Joseph who had successfully interpreted the former's dream in prison. Joseph was eventually presented before Pharaoh whose dreams he successfully interpreted while also proffering some solution for the problematic situation revealed through the interpretation. As a result, he was made a ruler in Egypt subsequently giving him authority over his siblings and father just as God had revealed to him in his dreams. (Joseph's father, Jacob, and the rest of his family would later relocate to Egypt where they found themselves under Joseph's authority.)

What this story reveals is that what God had decreed for Joseph (revealed to him in dreams) that he would someday have authority over members of his family — eventually was fulfilled after several twists and turns. The key point, however, is that it was fulfilled at the appointed time and although before its eventual fulfilment Joseph was exposed to a series of difficulties (and must've cried unto God for help), God still did not interfere with the timing of his decrees on behalf of Joseph but instead allowed it to pan out just as ordained because God respects his decrees and allows them to perform as ordained (including timing). I wouldn't suppose Joseph could've done anything at anytime which might've expedited the fulfilment of the vision he had in his dreams — the events were completely outside his sphere of influence so that he couldn't have influenced any of them no matter how hard he may have tried even if he could've tried. Every event, in the series of events that culminated in his promotion, could only happen at their respective appointed times. Let us now look at a few of those events:

- Joseph's brothers originally intended to kill him but eventually decided to sell him for money because, incidentally, they chanced upon some slave traders at the very time they would've killed him.
- The slave traders took Joseph to Egypt (not any other place).
- Joseph prospered in Potiphar's house before he was falsely accused, wrongly convicted and eventually imprisoned.
- In prison he was brought in contact with Pharaoh's chief butler, who apparently forgot about him after the latter's release from prison but later remembered him about two years later.
- Pharaoh had some dreams which no one else could accurately interpret and in the process Joseph was called upon to assist, which he did.

- Joseph went beyond only interpreting Pharaoh's dreams and proffered effective solutions for the problem the interpretation revealed — he wasn't required or expected to proffer solutions but he did. Why? Possibly, he simply felt prompted to do so. Again, why?
- Pharaoh didn't have to promote Joseph to the position of a ruler — there are many other ways he could've shown appreciation and gratitude for Joseph's assistance — but that was exactly what he did (possibly against normal protocols since Joseph could rightly be regarded an ex-convict and possibly also a refugee).

Now let us ponder how many of these events Joseph could've possibly influenced — both in occurrence as well as timing. Could Joseph, for instance, have been able in any way to do any of the following: Change the minds of his brothers? Take himself to Egypt as a slave? Orchestrated his meeting with Pharaoh's chief butler? Make Pharaoh have those dreams? Make it impossible for others to be able to correctly interpret Pharaoh's dreams? I suppose the answer to each of these questions is rather obvious — possibly not!

Let us now also consider how each of those events led one to the other (as if in a pre-planned definite order) such that one event had to first occur before the next could occur and so on until the climax. For instance, Joseph first had to be in Egypt and at a particular time (for that he was sold as a slave and his dealers brought him there); had to be somehow brought to the awareness of Pharaoh (for that he was imprisoned, Pharaoh's chief butler also had to be in prison where the both men met); and for him to be brought to the awareness of Pharaoh the latter had to have need for his services (for that Pharaoh had a dream which no one else could correctly interpret). Far from being a series of coincidences, it is more reasonable to believe that these events were all pre-planned and ordained well in advance of their actual occurrences.

Finally, and more significant to the particular issue under consideration — that of God allowing his decrees to perform as ordained — notice how these events all occurred at specific times — I suppose their respective appointed times — and also how God did not (out of e.g. compassion for Joseph due to the various dire straits in which he would find himself or in response to the numerous supplications which I suppose Joseph would've made unto God during his various ordeals) interfere with their timings. God allowed each event to occur at their right times and as planned.

(With respect to the self-fulfilling nature of God's decrees, note how those events occurred at particular times. For instance, how it was at a particular time that Pharaoh had his dream — not before his chief butler had been brought into contact with Joseph — and how it was at a particular time that the chief butler was imprisoned — not before Joseph was sent to prison and how it was at a particular time that Joseph's brothers decided to kill him — not before the slave traders were in their area or after they had left their area. As I already mentioned, I believe these things happened exactly when they did because it was the time appointed for them. I did also say that when the appointed time matures for the fulfilment of any of God's decrees the power of God's spoken word causes things to happen to orchestrate the fulfilment of the things spoken or decreed. And so I suppose Joseph's brothers, for instance, decided to kill him when they did as a result of the workings of the self-fulfilling nature of God's decrees. I suppose also Pharaoh had his dream when he did because the time had come for Joseph to be released into what God has decreed for him. Note finally that had God allowed Joseph the privilege of influencing the timings of the various events, it is very unlikely he would've got them right.)

In the end, it becomes very clear that God is honourable and he respects his decrees, allowing them to happen as and when planned.

God is responsible (and for all of his creation).

God is responsible — he never abandons or shirks his duties — and is primarily and ultimately responsible for the provision of the needs of every of his creation. God also assumes full responsibility for any of his actions.

The very order of creation reveals a meticulous and well-thought-out plan, designed in such a way that no particular creature was made before what it needed for its survival; instead every item of creation was made only after what it required for its existence has already been created. For instance, God first created light, in the midst of darkness, before then separating the light from the darkness to give cause to Day and Night; it was only after the creation of light God created the firmament, to separate the waters, thereby giving cause to Heaven. Note that in total darkness, creating Heaven would have made little or no sense as it would've been invisible and so unrecognisable: it needed to be visible to be appreciated, so God first made the light before making the heavens. Similarly, it was only after separating the waters from the waters God gathered the waters under the heaven unto one place, giving cause to dry land. (Where would've dry land been placed had not the firmament first been created to mark a distinction between upwards and downwards? Land or earth couldn't just hang lopsided or simply suspended in the ozone layer without any solid base, or it wouldn't be fit for purpose.) Also, it was only after the Earth was created that God commanded it to bring forth all types of vegetation; because those vegetation would require dry land for their existence. Note also that it was only after the creation of vegetation that God created the many creatures that live in the water and that fly above the earth, all of whom would depend on vegetation for their existence. So that by the time fishes or birds, for instance, were created there was already in existence the food (different types of plants and micro-organisms) they would depend on for their sustenance. And so on…, until humans were created; after everything they would require for sustenance — foods (plants and animals), water, light, shelter (dry lands, and vegetations from which shelter can be built, etc.), and much later, clothing (from animals, e.g. skins, wools, etc. and plants, e.g. dyes, etc.) — had already been created; and whom God put in charge over the rest of his creation.

By creating us, God has automatically assumed responsibility for us and all other creations; a truth which is reflected in the following statement made by Jesus Christ:

> Therefore I say unto you, Take no thought for your life, what ye shall eat, or what ye shall drink; nor yet for your body, what

ye shall put on. Is not the life more than meat, and the body than raiment?

Behold the fowls of the air: for they sow not, neither do they reap, nor gather into barns; yet your heavenly Father feedeth them. Are ye not much better than they?

Which of you by taking thought can add one cubit unto his stature?

And why take ye thought for raiment? Consider the lilies of the field, how they grow; they toil not, neither do they spin:

And yet I say unto you, That even Solomon in all his glory was not arrayed like one of these.

Wherefore, if God so clothe the grass of the field, which to day is, and to morrow is cast into the oven, shall he not much more clothe you, O ye of little faith?

Therefore take no thought, saying, What shall we eat? or, What shall we drink? or, Wherewithal shall we be clothed?

(Matthew 6:25-31;KJV)

I suppose we could simply summarise the above as: God who gave life is able to sustain it. And God does truly sustain each life he has brought into existence, never shirking any of his responsibilities and never abandoning any of his creation. To demonstrate this attribute of God's — responsible and responsibility — we shall look at a few examples, starting with the story of prophet Elijah (Details can be found in I Kings 17:1 - 16):

At a time when there was a severe drought in Israel — occasioned by prophetic pronouncements by Elijah — God expressly instructed Elijah to go directly to a specific brook (called Cherith) to reside there; so that he could drink from the brook, while also informing the latter that he has commanded the ravens to feed him there. And so it was that every morning and evening the ravens would bring Elijah bread and flesh, and he drank from the brook. After a while, however, the brook dried up — because there had been no rain in the land — and so God, again, expressly instructed Elijah to go to a place called Zarephath (in Zidon) to reside; while also informing the latter that he has commanded a certain widow there to sustain him. (Note that the brook, Cherith, dried up because there had been no rain in the land and that there had been no rain in the land because Elijah had commanded so. And so here again we see God not willing to interfere with nature; because although God could sustain the brook without rainfall (had he wanted to), he instead allowed nature to run its course, so that in the absence of rainfall the brook dried up quite naturally.)

It so happened that as Elijah arrived at Zarephath he met the widow in question; having initially requested for a drink of water, he almost immediately followed it up with a request for a proper meal and although this widow would initially object to his latter request (for the simple reason that she had very limited supplies), she eventually did provide Elijah with a meal as requested. Elijah assured her — based on God's instructions to him — that her supplies would not run out till the day that God will again send rain to the land.

The main thing to note here, is how God assumed the responsibility for providing for Elijah:

- Plans were made in advance of these provisions.
- Specific instructions (including particular locations, persons or things involved) were made available to Elijah.
- Despite the severity of the circumstances — drought, limited supplies, famine — provisions were made available.

The other example relates to the children of Israel — during their journey through the wilderness. (Details can be found in Exodus 15 - 16) The nascent nation of Israel, journeyed for about forty years through the wilderness; because of the transient nature of each of their stops during their journey, they could not effectively engage in their normal occupations. Consequently, very early in that journey, they would run out of the food supplies they had brought with them from Egypt. And so, God provided them with quails and something else which looked like wafers, which they called "manna", to last them for the entire duration of their journey.

This story also helps to demonstrate that God is always responsible: He wouldn't shirk any of his duties, is always reliable and also dependable.

In relating with God therefore, it is important that we recognise and acknowledge this attribute of his which consequently, could help to relieve us from unnecessary and avoidable stress.

In addition to the above, we also ought to ensure that we seek divine guidance with respect to the provision of our needs and, more importantly, to comply with the instructions and directives we might receive. On this very last point — compliance with divine instructions — let us see how the children of Israel fared during this particular journey in reference. They were given a specific instruction:

> This is the thing which the Lord hath commanded, **Gather of it every man according to his eating**, an omer for every man, according to the number of your persons; take ye every man for them which are in his tents. (Exodus 16:16;KJV)

In plainer terms, each person was required to gather only as much as was necessary to satisfy his or her needs (not wants or greed). But did they all comply?

> And the children of Israel did so, and gathered, **some more, some less**. (Exodus 16:17;KJV)

Well they didn't! And then this happens:

> And when they did **mete it with an omer, he that gathered much had nothing over, and he that gathered little had no lack;** they gathered every man according to his eating. (Exodus 16:18;KJV)

Imagine that! A bit mysterious, not so? But this is only half of the mystery as there is still one more intrigue to come:

> And Moses said, **Let no man leave of it till the morning**. (Exodus 16:19;KJV)

In plainer terms, do not worry about tomorrow — by trying to provide for tomorrow from today's provisions — I suppose because each day has its own provisions. Again, did they comply with this simple instruction?

> Notwithstanding they hearkened not unto Moses; **but some of them left of it until the morning**, and it bred worms, and stank: and Moses was wroth with them. (Exodus 16:20;KJV)

Classic! It is most likely that those who left some of the manna over till the next morning did so for either of two reasons — (1) they gathered more than they could consume that day (i.e. excessive accumulation) or (2) they tried to save some for the next day (i.e. saving for the rainy days, as it were) — but whatever their reasons, no matter how humanly sensible or prudent their judgements were, the result was simply the same — their efforts, plans, and expectations amounted to nothing. It was all in vain because the manna which was leftover got wasted. Please note that their efforts amounted to nothing not because they weren't reasonable, prudent, or sensible but simply because they acted contrary to divine instructions. (Which somehow further confirms that we are not primarily responsible for ourselves; because had it been we are then their efforts would've been rewarded differently, it wouldn't have been fair that after toiling to store away some manna these people would wake up to discover them wasted.)

And just to prove that manna could last more than a day — meaning that the leftovers this particular time got spoilt as a result of disobedience — when on the sixth day they gathered twice their daily requirements — as instructed, because the next day was a holy day, Sabbath — the extras remained fresh, unspoilt and fit for consumption on the day after. Would you believe, however, that even on the Sabbath day of rest, some of them still went out in search of manna (after having been instructed to gather twice their daily requirements on the day before because manna would not fall on the Sabbath day)? So, when they were required to gather less, some of them gathered more; and when required to gather more, some of them gathered less — disobedience — with the result that such people were left disappointed in the end.

Final verdict: They obviously didn't fare very well.

Sadly, it may surprise you that some of us might be repeating the same mistakes some of these Israelites made during their journey: It is possible some people accumulate more than they really need; it is also possible some people sometimes or often do engage themselves in other unnecessary and fruitless endeavours. For instance, some people might be toiling where and when they ought not to (just like the Israelites who went seeking for manna on the Sabbath day, whereas they should've gathered extras, as instructed, the day before to cater for the holy day of rest) or some other people might be very busy toiling in preparation for rainy days which may never come, meaning that their accumulations could in the end be in vain. Compliance with divine instructions, however, would relieve us of unproductive efforts and would also guarantee us better lives.

Before we could comply with instructions, however, we need to first receive them; for us to receive them, we need to first seek them. We are more likely to seek divine help, including instructions and directives, with respect to the provision of our needs when we thoroughly appreciate the fact that God, and not ourselves, is primarily responsible for all of our needs.

God is Love.

God is love; love governs everything God does — we were created because of God's love, his dealings with us are entirely out of love.

> He that loveth not knoweth not God; **for God is love**. (I John 4:8;KJV)

Love, I suppose, is the overarching attribute of God's, because everything God is (and does) revolves around love. For instance, it is out of love the Lord God created Adam and Eve — whom he placed in charge of all other creations; which were actually created for the overall benefit of the two humans. It is because of his love for us that God did not immediately destroy Adam and Eve the moment they transgressed his commandments, but instead made atonement for their transgression thereby restoring them to himself and to his protection. Throughout human history, we can easily observe this love at play in many different ways including the eventual arrival of God the Son on earth in human form in the person of Jesus Christ, who laid down his life as a sacrifice for the atonement of our sins.

On a personal level, love — God's love — is responsible for our individual existence: God has a plan for every one of us and that plan is designed in love and for love.

> For I know the thoughts that I think toward you, saith the Lord, thoughts of peace, and not of evil, to give you an expected end. (Jeremiah 29:11;KJV)

This is the summation of God's plans for us — a very good and happy life.

One of the best things about God's love is that it is unconditional — it is wholesome, complete, guaranteed, limitless, and with no strings attached. God loves every one of us equally — regardless of whether we live our lives in accordance to his desires and plans for us or not — and there is nothing we could do to make him love us more — simply because he already loves each of us maximally and limitlessly — or to love us less — because his love never changes or diminishes, even if we life in ways that are contrary to his expectations for us. God loves us whether we love him back or not; I suppose just as God honours his decrees and wouldn't arbitrarily interfere with them regardless of circumstances, his love for every of his creations also remains unchanged regardless.

To help demonstrate the unconditional nature of God's love let us consider the following:

- All humans (whether considered good or bad) are exposed to the same circumstances (e.g. sicknesses, problems, difficult situations, trials, persecutions, etc.)
- The sun shines on all, the rain falls upon all the lands, and people prosper regardless of how they live their lives.

- God protects all from all forms of dangers (including those encountered as a result of living contrary to his wishes).
- God provides for the needs of all.

God never discriminates, is not partisan, not partial or biased, and he is always fair to all on an equal basis. (Sadly, we humans are not like God, in many respects including his unconditional love for all. We are the ones who sometimes love others conditionally, discriminate, are prejudiced, partial, biased, and often unfair (even to ourselves). Most times also we are unfair to God: blaming him for what he is not responsible for (most of which we might actually be responsible for), taking him for granted, and often failing to respect him.)

The attributes highlighted in the chapter are few and very limited, but I believe they would help in contributing to a better understanding of who God exactly is. It would be impossible understanding everything about God but if we can understand him enough as to have a proper, effective and productive relationship with him then such understanding will do, no matter how limited they may be.

Chapter 11

A new me

We have so far come a very long way since we started our journey, which we commenced at birth: where we encountered a few of life's mysteries — why our conception occurred when and how it did; why our birth occurred when, where and how it did — before making a brief detour via the exciting journey-within-a-journey of self-discovery, where we explored the who and why of our individual existence.

Emerging from our adventure in self-discovery, we tried to refocus our bearing on the main journey and so we tried plotting our coordinates. Having established our coordinates — where from and where to — we then advanced into the journey proper: encountering the various birth circumstances and upbringings that could've made us the persons we have become — we explored how our different family and educational systems, and other societal influences we might've been exposed to as we progressed from childhood into adulthood could've contributed largely in moulding us into the different persons we might've become.

During this stage of the journey, we witnessed how we might've been exposed to different mindsets, depending on our particular birth circumstances and upbringings. We had a good look at the competitive mindset, which possibly most people are exposed to from early childhood — meaning that we might've become self-centred, selfish, competitive and might regard other people as rivals (instead of partners); in which case, we might also have presumed that the only way to succeed in life would be by outperforming our contemporaries. We also went on an interesting excursion, which took us through the many streets and avenues of our minds: here we also discovered how our minds might've become subjected to external controls and influences, in more than a few ways (e.g. at our homes, at the various educational institutions we have been a part of, and later, at our various workplaces as well), and how we might've become more dependent on being told what to do instead of trying to originally figure out for ourselves how to do. We discovered that we might've not been applying our minds in thinking independently and originally but instead might've often thought as guided or conditioned. The need to think — independently — was emphasised and was pointed out as what makes us individuals. We were also informed that there may be a few inventions or innovations waiting to be discovered were we to engage our minds independently and originally.

As the journey progressed, we were brought in contact with several other people, most of whom we had never met before, but all of whom we had to relate with in one form or another. We then reflected on how best to conduct our different relationships and interactions with these people whom we have encountered: here we discussed love, and were made to understand that we ought to love and treat other people as we would expect others to love and treat us. We were reminded that it was a duty we owed ourselves — to love and treat others as we would expect others to love and treat us — because we are all interconnected and interrelated. Furthermore, we all have a common origin; to help demonstrate this fact, we explored our origin where we discovered that we all share a common ancestry — in the first man and woman, Adam and Eve — and that our more recent ancestors first originated in Africa before migrating to other parts of the world. During this stage of the journey, we also explored the many classifications and categorisations with which we have been divided (e.g. black, white, nationalities, ethnicities, tribes, social classes, etc.) and also how our divisions are responsible for most of the problems we have subsequently encountered (e.g. slavery, colonisation, wars, holocausts, genocides, diseases, poverty, famines, etc.). As we tried to further explore these categorisations and classifications, trying to understand their basis and relevance, we were perplexed at how it was very easy for people who were at one time classified as "them" to subsequently and effortlessly qualify as "we"; we also found it very hard keeping up with the consistent inconsistencies which characterised these divisions. At a point it became difficult telling who was a "we" and who was a "them", which made us wonder if indeed there should be a "we" and "them". Perplexed and confused as we were, we had no choice but to plod on and on into the highways of life.

And plodding on we did, until we came across the islands of treasures where we discovered treasures — money, wealth, riches and other material possessions — and, almost instantly, also discovered that money rules. On closer scrutiny, however, we observed that money was just a means to an end — bundles of paper — and that our various needs are indeed the real ends; meaning that our needs should be our primary focus, and not the accumulation of excess wealth. While still on these islands, we looked on curiously as we saw some people pursuing money so hard and so much that they didn't have the time to even enjoy the money they were making and amassing. We saw people who complicated what should've been a simple and happy life, as a result of their misplaced priorities, making life almost unbearable and meaningless. And so we were left bemused and a tad perplexed.

It was at this stage in the journey that we realised we needed some form of assistance — either in the form of proper directions or a reliable guide as it somehow appeared that we were just going round in circles. Consequently, we ventured into the minefields of contemporary religion — in search of the right way — where having wobbled, staggered, and stumbled through its webbed and confusing network of roads (almost getting lost in the maze) we, fortunately, eventually found a clear and safe path, which was void of the dangers and loopholes prevalent in those minefields — the only path through which we might continue our journey with a guaranteed successful and victorious completion and subsequent arrival at our eternal destination. Home, sweet home.

It was while walking on this path that we found our creator — God Almighty — the only reliable guide; whom we found to be omnipotent, omniscient, omnipresent, reliable, responsible, and loving. We were then reminded of the need and importance of relating with God, especially since he is the only person who can successfully lead us home.

And so, at this stage of the journey — after such a long walk — we now have the much-deserved (and I guess, much-awaited also) opportunity to pull over so as to observe a quick "comfort break" before embarking on the rest, and concluding, part of the journey. During this break, we would be having another very close look at ourselves (almost similar to our earlier adventure in self-discovery) but this time to assess how the journey so far might've affected us. We shall be looking at the new us — A new me — the individuals which we ought to have become after all that we have encountered through the journey so far; possibly the individuals we were originally intended to be.

Who ought you to be? — The new you.

The person we are each supposed to be should at least possess some of the qualities or attributes which make a human being human. Some of these basic human characteristics — the things that should qualify a person as a human being — are as follows:

A free mind.

Every human being is born equipped with a mind, the primary and basic function of which is to think. Thinking, however, should be original and independent if it is to serve its true purpose — helping us discover or assess things as we ought to — otherwise if thinking becomes influenced, guided, conditioned or controlled in any ways and to any degrees then it can no longer be said to be a due process of reasoning; it simply would then have become a mere compliance process — where people think as expected and possibly for an expected outcome.

As an individual, you should not only be able to think, but you should also always think through all the things you are presented with (e.g. philosophies, ideologies, concepts, information, etc.) so as to personally and independently ascertain the authenticity, accuracy, truthfulness, completeness, sincerity, or objectiveness of those things regardless of their sources. You were made to think — and to think for yourself and originally — hence you were created with your own mind. Had it been God had designed that only a proportion of humanity should think — for themselves and others — I suppose we would've been created such that only some people are born equipped with minds while the others are left with none. That way those people born without minds could then rightly depend on the others who have minds to assist them with thinking. But since we are all born each with his or her own mind, it seems rather obvious we are all expected to use our minds and to use them independently.

Remember that as powerful as the human mind is, it is also very fragile and easily manipulatable; that by being able to influence our minds, we can also easily be controlled by the sources of such external influences.

Our minds can be exposed to various degrees of external control; they can also be exposed to various forms of control: depending on the extent to which our minds have been subjected to any forms of control, depending also on how many forms of control we are exposed to, our lives could be lives which are largely controlled or conditioned. Consequently, we ought to take due care in ensuring our minds are relatively free of any forms of external control. We need to be sure the things we believe to be true are indeed true; the things we strongly uphold as facts are indeed facts; our various judgements (including the opinions we uphold about other people, places and things) are unbiased, fair and correctly informed; our sense of propriety is not based on popular or generally-upheld definitions alone but on personal convictions; we do things because we really want to and not because others are doing same; and, generally, that we live the lives we really want to live and not lives we presume we should live, based on societal or peer influences.

To be able to do all of the above (and possibly more) we definitely need to first free our minds of any possible present external influences — we need a fresh mind. And having done that to constantly and continuously ensure that our minds remain void of undue external influences — free!

A unique person.

Every individual is made in a special and unique way — we do not have any exact replicas; although people sometimes do share a few common traits (e.g. physical features, mannerisms, personalities, mental capabilities, etc.), we nonetheless are never the same as others. There is only one copy of each of us, which is what makes each of us rare masterpieces.

Since God created us as unique individuals, it would be reasonable to presume that he did that for a reason: possibly, God expects us to live our own lives — as individuals — in the unique ways he has created us. Had God designed us to exist as masses he probably would've made us all similar so that we couldn't be told apart. But since we are all different and unique, it sounds reasonable believing that we also are designed to live uniquely and differently too.

Remember that each of us is created for a special purpose — why you are here — which only each of us can fulfil; for that reason, we are made the way we are — who you are — as a one and only copy, with no replicas or duplicates. Consequently, we ought to ensure that we become who we are created to be and that we perform the things we are created to perform. To be able to accomplish both we need to look inwards — to self — and not outwards — to others. We cannot become who we are created to be by imitating other people, copying the lifestyles of others, trying to adapt to the standards of others and, generally, neglecting our uniqueness while trying to make ourselves the same as others. Similarly, we couldn't possibly fulfil our purposes if constantly we do the things others are doing, aspire for the achievements others have made, try to accomplish the same things others have accomplished, have the same ambitions others have and, generally, if we set our aims, objectives and standards based on others.

We would then be void of genuine personal dreams — wherein lies our purposes — but would instead settle for the dreams of others — which often are elusive, because we probably are not created with what is needed to realise them (because they are not ours).

We can all be better versions of ourselves (if we try), but we could never be any version of someone else (try hard as we may). And so instead of engaging in an exercise in futility — in trying to be like others — we could engage ourselves more productively by trying to become more and more of who we are meant to be. Focusing on becoming who we are created to be, pursuing those things we are created for, would also benefit our lives immeasurably in other ways: we would be relieved of the debilitating competitive mindset with all its negative consequences, also of the overbearing weight of peer and societal pressures, with the result that our lives would become less stressful and more positive and enjoyable.

The new you should be the real you; it is unique — it is that uniqueness that makes you you.

Purpose-driven.

We are all created for a purpose — why we are here and each life assumes its true meaning and significance only when lived in accordance with that purpose.

Remember, when no use or usefulness can be found for something, that thing is considered useless or worthless; that before anything is made, a particular need or purpose must've warranted its making (we don't make things just for the sake of making them) or else it probably wouldn't have been made. Consequently, a thing would become truly useful only when it is applied for the purpose it was made and which necessitated its making in the first place. Otherwise, a wrong application could generally undermine its usefulness; it could also mean that that thing might suffer one form of abuse or another, both of which would greatly affect it negatively.

It means then our true existence lies in living a life driven by the purpose for which we are created — we truly exist only when we live as designed. To live a purpose-driven life, however, we much first discover our purposes; and having discovered our purposes to pursue them as best we can. I believe that living as designed and for our designs would greatly enrich our lives in many ways just as applying an object for its right use makes life easy both for the object and for the person using it. For instance, it is easier to use a car to get from one place to another than to live inside it; it is easier hewing down a tree with an axe than with a razor blade; it is more comfortable sitting on a chair than standing on it; it is also more comfortable walking about in shoes than in roller blades.

Living becomes relatively easier when things are done as they should be; our lives also become easier when lived in accordance with their purposes. When we find the right use for ourselves — purpose — we also find meanings for our lives and our lives become more worth living. A life without a meaning is a hapless and boring one, and one often filled with disillusionment. It could also be a disaster waiting to happen: some people end their lives only because they wrongly believe they are worthless and their lives no longer worth living. Imagine having to wake up every morning with no plans, goals, objectives, or things to do and if that happens to be the case for the foreseeable future — would you look forward to living? Imagine also having to constantly and continuously engage in fruitless endeavours or pursuits (such that it seems in most cases you are simply going round in circles but making no tangible progress or headway) which often leaves you unsatisfied or fulfilled, possibly because you have been doing the things not meant for you (your purpose) — would you be happy?

We are not created to pursue fame and fortune; we are created for something more. Fame and fortune are only by-products but they are definitely not the main goal. Fame and fortune cannot guarantee happiness or satisfaction in life, both can only become meaningful as well as beneficial when they come as a result of our doing the things we are created to do.

To truly live we have to live in accordance to our purposes; it is only the real you, however, who can live in line with what you are created for. It means the new you — the who — has to be driven by the purpose of your creation — the why.

Unconditional love.

One thing which happens to be common with all humans, is the ability to love, and to love naturally — we don't have to learn to love before we could love, instead loving is something which comes naturally to us all. We are created in love, and because of love, so living becomes more satisfying and meaningful when we live a life of love. I could possibly say that love is a basic ingredient in our constitution and creation. And maybe the main ingredient.

Love is the hub to which all of life's other fragments are attached, without it life couldn't really function effectively and properly. Love brings people from different backgrounds, circumstances and ethnic origins together, uniting them into one homogeneous whole so that there are no distinctions but just a single entity — human beings. In the absence of love, it would almost be impracticable for humanity to exist and to coexist because most of the other ingredients necessary for human relationships, associations and coexistence (e.g. trust, selflessness, honesty, sincerity, loyalty, kindness, respect, friendliness, etc.) are all somewhat assisted by love. (Seeing then how important and necessary loving one another is, it is rather sad that to a greater extent we are encouraged to love discriminately, by choosing who to benefit with our love and who not to, often based on perceived differences. It would seem that we often place more emphasis on those classifications with which we have been divided instead of on those things we all have in common, so that instead of coming together we unwittingly tear ourselves apart. But who really stands to gain from a divided and disunited world?)

Because we are made with love and to love, we need to love if we are to truly live. We are meant to love one another (as we love ourselves) and to seek our collective best interests, instead of individual selfish interests. And so to truly qualify as humans, we ought to love ourselves and others the very way we were meant to — unconditionally. I suppose since God loves us unconditionally, we couldn't really be expected to love in any other way. Loving unconditionally could mean that we do things not only for our benefit but also for the benefit of others — it shouldn't be about us alone but about everyone else. For instance, when we assist someone it should be because such a person needs the assistance and not necessarily because he or she deserves it. We should also not assist someone in order to make ourselves feel good, or so as to make the beneficiary of our assistance feel or become indebted to us; we should do so only because it is the right thing to do. Similarly, love has to be genuine for it to be effective and productive, otherwise it couldn't possibly serve the right purpose.

The truth is that when we love others we actually are doing ourselves more good, because the satisfaction we derive from treating other people with love is priceless. The quality of our lives could greatly be improved as a result of treating ourselves and others right.

And so, the new you ought to love; to love genuinely and unconditionally.

A living spirit.

The presence of a spirit is probably what makes us human; it possibly also is the main characteristic which distinguishes us from the rest of creation. In the absence of our spirits, we would be mere lifeless bodies; the significant thing about the human spirit is that it came from the breath of life — God's breath.

We have already been made aware that a spirit disconnected from God — the source of our spirits — could be said to be merely existing but not living, as such a spirit is largely existing in a dormant state. Dormancy is characterised by limited or stunted growth and relative inactivity — meaning that a dormant spirit would largely be underutilised and its potentials not fully tapped. Dormancy can be illustrated thus: when an electrical appliance (e.g. a TV set, stereo, electric kettle, etc.) is unplugged or disconnected from a power source, in which case it is largely of little or no use and cannot be effectively applied for its right purpose. In that unplugged state the TV set, for instance, is merely existing as a box or piece of furniture (with no real utility), even though it possesses almost every quality that makes it a TV set and could actually pass for a TV set. When plugged to a power source, however, it ceases to merely exist as an item of furniture and begins to live the life a TV should live, thereby becoming useful.

Dormancy of the spirit is probably one of our biggest problems: It renders us inactive and of limited usefulness, but worse than that is it also makes us vulnerable to other rogue spirits who being without a body constantly are on the look out for bodies that they could operate from or through. It is possible for evil spirits to attach themselves to people whose spirits have been left dormant, thereby either possessing such people or occupying their bodies at will and when needed. And so we may be relating with fellow human beings not knowing that some of their actions are not necessarily theirs but instead could be outward expressions occasioned by other spirit influences who have access to and use of such people. We may, for instance, witness some people committing heinous crimes (e.g. serial killings, mass murders, gross sexual abuses or violation of others, etc.) and wonder how a human being could do such things. It may be that some of such people have allowed themselves to become useable by evil spirits, a situation which is possible when a person's spirit is unconnected to its source and therefore is dormant.

It then means that for us to live our lives to the fullest our spirits must be alive and active. Our spirits can only be alive when connected to source — connected to God through a personal and direct relationship which would enable a constant and continuous association and interaction between us and the source of our spiritual nourishment (God). Even a presently-dormant spirit can be brought back to life quite easily by a simple reconnection with God just as it is very easy to cause a TV set to perform as a TV should by simply plugging it to a power source and switching it on.

A new you would possess a living spirit — one connected to God.

Life

These are only a few characteristics of who we ought to be — the real us; the new us — but I suppose by the time we acquire them we would've been properly equipped to discover everything else that is part of who we ought to be.

Remember: Only the real you can live the life you were created to live; also, only by living the life you were created to live would you find fulfilment.

A new you would mean a new life, and a new world.

Chapter 12

A brand new world

The world would be a different place when you become a different person; so, a changed people would result in a changed world — a brand new world. The world we now live in is essentially a result of our designs, choices and preferences; however, we are also a product of the world we found ourselves in, as it largely contributed to making us who we have become — one of the paradoxes of life, I guess.

We made the world what it now is. And what world might that be?

The world today.

Below is a summary of the highlights of the world we have made:

- The world is now greatly divided into various parts, based on many different criteria. The world today is divided into continents, with each continent further divided into different countries, and each country further divided along the lines of different nationalities, tribes or ethnicities. And even within nations, tribes or ethnic groups, there are also still many further subdivisions which themselves continue to be further divided up until the family stage, which is equally further divided into nuclear families.

- The world is also now categorised and classified into undeveloped, under-developed, developing and developed, but all existing as part of the same world — which is almost akin to describing a person as having strong legs, weak hands, stunted neck, and poorly sighted; a bit unrealistic and confusing because it is either a person is healthy or he or she is not healthy, breaking him or her into parts which are qualified based on their individual strengths and weaknesses almost seems like child's play. The world is then further classified into civilised and non-civilised, and also rich and poor — a rather dubious thing because in some so-called rich countries, there exist individual poverty at significant levels enough to undermine or question this classification; while in some so-called poor countries there also exist individual affluence at an equally significant levels enough to make rubbish of the classification. Similarly, as has been shown by historical facts, civilisation has long been experienced, in some of the places now classified as non-civilised, even before some of the so-called civilised parts of the world began to experience their own brands of civilisation. Furthermore, present definition of civilisation seems to ignore the fact that civilisation is both dynamic as well as diverse such that it could not rightly be subjected to the same or a single set of criteria or yardsticks. Different cultures do things differently; as a result, advancement in the ways things are done — civilisation — is unique and indigenous with respect to different cultures; one culture cannot then be rightly compared with another since they are all different.
- The world we have designed is one divided on the basis of the colours of our skins, so that instead of a single human race (as it truly is and so should be) we now have the so-called black and white races. Within each of the two main races, however, the division continues as there are further reclassifications. It is also a world divided along the lines of our contemporary religions, each of which is further subdivided into various denominations, or sects, and which themselves are further subsequently subdivided.

Consequently:

- We have a world filled with multitudes of people but not enough individuals; everyone tries to be like everyone else — thinking and behaving alike, and also aspiring for the same things.
- We have a world in competition with itself, with everyone jostling against one another in order to emerge at the top or to do better than the others.
- We have a world where love is subjective and unconditional love simply an ideal — an utopia — but not something considered practicable or possible.
- We have a world ruled by money — material wealth and possessions — so that instead of controlling and managing it, money controls and manages us. We have allowed money to become an end, instead of the means to an end which it rightly is. As a result, we now have more money but less values, spend more but possess little, we acquire more but enjoy less, have bigger cars but lone passengers, have huge mansions but tiny families, and no matter how much we have we are never satisfied and so we want more.
- We have a world filled with many educated people who turn out to be common illiterates, more academic qualifications and certificates but fewer common sense, multitude of intelligent people but only a few wise ones, people who are well informed but possess limited knowledge, and a world where many claim to be experts yet our problems keep multiplying.
- We have a world with different religions; filled with many religious people but very few godly persons, people who claim to know God yet deny his very existence, people who confess daily that life on earth is transient but live as though it will never end, people who say one thing and do another, who say what they don't mean and don't mean what they say, people who constantly proclaim peace but consistently engage in wars, people who outwardly appear very confident of their beliefs but inwardly are torn apart with doubt, confusions and uncertainties, many self-appointed masters and

leaders who themselves were disciples to none; a world whose many religions would instead of reconnecting you with God will instead prevent you from knowing him.

This is our world today. The world we have made is a world in desperate need of a makeover; a makeover which we can accomplish because it was us who reduced the world to its current state. But that is, if and when we decide the status quo is no longer tenable and that we need a change.

There could be a better world; we can make our world that better world. What better world could there be?

The world that could be.

- The world that could be is an undivided world void of classifications, categorisations and distinctions. It is a world whose inhabitants cohabit and coexist as one, living in love, peace and unity, working for the mutual benefit of all. Going by the composition and constitution of the world it would seem that was how God intended it to be — a place whose inhabitants coexist harmoniously and interdependently, with the people in its different parts fulfilling specific and different roles and functions (required for its sustenance) in a perfect cooperation — because he created the world in such a way that different natural resources are found in different parts of the world such that no single part or region possesses every available natural resources, meaning that the different parts of the world would have to depend on each other for some of their resources needs.

And so, while we may find crude oil and other petroleum resources exclusively or predominantly in certain parts of the world (e.g. in some West African countries, notably Nigeria; Middle East Asia, notably Saudi Arabia and other Gulf States; and North America, notably Texas in the United States of America), we may also find certain metals and minerals exclusively or predominantly in other parts of the world (e.g. chromium — Turkey, titanium — Norway, silver — Poland), or natural gas in other parts (e.g. Europe, notably Russia, Netherlands and United Kingdom).

Having to depend on other regions for one or more resources should naturally engender a mutual relationship between the different regions, which in turn would foster unity. And so it would seem that God intended the world to be undivided but united.

- The world that could be is a unified (though diverse) global family, with every part of that family jointly contributing to and benefiting from the union in a proportionate and fair manner. (A good analogy here could be the human body, which though consists of many different parts — some hidden, some in outward display, some very minute (and invisible to the naked eye), others very big, some (e.g. the heart) performing very crucial roles, others (e.g. the appendix) performing seemingly less crucial roles — can only function effectively only when all its parts work together in perfect harmony.)

Similarly, we should acknowledge and appreciate our different endowments and capabilities while appreciating that each part of the world has a specific role; that the world could only function effectively when every part plays their respective roles.

- The world that could be is a world whose inhabitants are not categorized and branded (much like branded products) based on the colours of their skins; it is a world where there is neither black, white, red or yellow but just human beings and just a single race — human race.

Consequently, there would be no need for one "brand" of people to constantly try to dehumanise, disparage, intimidate, dominate and manipulate another "brand"; nor would there be any need for one group of people to constantly live in fear and apprehension of another group of people.

- It is a world whose trading is conducted in fairness, so that resources are given the value they deserve regardless of what part of the world they are found; where exchanges are conducted in fairness, so that resources are exchanged on equal measures and value regardless of who is exchanging what and with whom; where trading partners are not coerced, intimidated or manipulated to trade or risk dubious sanctions and penalties; where prices are fairly and evenly determined by market forces and not arbitrarily fixed by a group of traders (to protect selfish interests); where the natural laws of demand and supply govern its activities.

Consequently, every part of the world would experience tangible, genuine and even development meaning that there wouldn't be the need for any parts of the world to rely on spurious handouts and so-called foreign aids from other parts of the world.

- The world that could be is one in which the sovereignty of its different parts are acknowledged and respected by all so that no parts experience any degree of incursions, invasions and interferences (especially with respect to natural and other resources) from other parts in whatever form or disguise or by whatever kindly or grand names they may be called.

Consequently, there will be peace in the different parts of the world and there would be no need for wars and other forms of violence.

- It is a world where in each of its counterpart regions, states or countries indigenes are treated equally in every respect, so that each group of people within a broader group benefits equally and proportionately from the resources in their locality.

Consequently, there would be no need for insurrections, breakaways and secessions.

- The world that could be is a world where people in different generations are encouraged and allowed to think for themselves (outside the box), as individuals, so that with each generation ideologies, philosophies and knowledge could be developed, originally, from its respective population (which I suppose could be the main reason they were born in their particular generation in the first place), as applicable and useful to them.

Consequently, successive generations are not left stuck back in times long past, by continuing to uphold, e.g. dated idioms, maxims, ideologies, or engaging in the pursuit of knowledge that might no longer be relevant in their times.

- The world that could be is a world where each person acknowledges and respects his or her uniqueness and realises that life is not a competition; we all have different unique purposes and destinies, which in turn determine most of our birth and other circumstances, privileges and opportunities.

Consequently, we would not strive in vain to outdo one another or to be like others, instead we would help one another as we all try to become the best of who we ought to be; also we would pull our personal and group resources together to try and achieve a common goal — a better quality of life for all and a better world — instead of selfishly pursuing personal interests, thereby availing ourselves of the synergies that we have so ignorantly been missing out on. Consequently also, our lives will become more meaningful, satisfying and fulfilling and we will then be able to enjoy and not endure living.

- The world that could be is one where money is not adored, worshipped and overrated; is not considered an end in itself but instead is seen as a means to an end (as it rightly is); that it has no intrinsic value except the value of what it is used in exchange for.

Consequently, we would not be constantly engaged in destroying our lives, its enjoyment and happiness, in the pursuit of more money than we need.

- It is a world united in love and honesty, with all of humanity understanding that we have only one enemy — evil — so that in all things and at all times we keep focus on the real enemy and not on ourselves.

Consequently, we would not risk imploding as we ignorantly fight against ourselves; we may then stand a better chance of defeating the real enemy: when we combat the real enemy we stand a good chance of winning but if we are misguided to fight the wrong enemy we not only risk losing but we also risk being destroyed.

- The world that could be is one in total sync with its maker, whose inhabitants endeavour to engage in honest, sincere and personal (as well as communal) relationships with God Almighty, whom they worship in spirit and in truth.

Consequently, we would not have the need (or be misguided) to worship fellow human beings, recreational activities or fictional objects and characters (in whatever form or to whatever degree) none of whom could truly satisfy the deeper longings of our souls but who could take advantage of our ignorance-fuelled obsessions to feed their vain ego while subtly lording it over us and also further enriching themselves with our individual contributions as we patronise their respective brands.

(It is very instructive to note that those individuals who consciously court the limelight seeking fame and adulation from fellow humans are themselves equally in pursuit of that real satisfaction for that inner vacuum only a true relationship with God Almighty can satisfy. More so, hugging fame is akin to riding the fictional ferocious and ravenous tiger, whose riders almost always end up destroyed and eaten by it; so choosing to exist in the limelight under constant scrutiny of the public also has its own additional peculiar dangers.)

It is because we are created with a natural inclination to relate with our maker — a process through which our spirits receive nourishment — that failing to truly worship the Creator (in ways that would satisfy our natural inclination to worship) we are subconsciously drawn to other objects (e.g. celebrities, sports and sporting events, music and musical events, fictional heroes and characters, etc.) as we seek in vain to fill the vacuum created as a result of our failing to worship God as we are supposed. If we worshipped God in spirit and in truth, the deeper longings of our souls would be truly satisfied and we would not have the need to seek satisfaction elsewhere.

Consequently also — by having a relationship with our maker in spirit and in truth — we would find true meaning, relevance and purpose to our existence; we would also be rightly guided on how best to navigate the journey of life so that we could make the most out of life.

The list could be endless, but suffice it to say that the world that could be is the world that was created to be — and the world that should be.

The world which should be might seem a bit utopian, and possibly, unattainable; but the one thing which is certain is that if we do not try we may never know. The world would not change itself and if we fail to do something different it would simply remain as it is now. But perhaps, if we did something (no matter how little) it might go a long way in bringing about some change. Anything could be considered impossible until it is done.

On that positive note, we shall now resume our journey as our comfort break is now over.

Part Three

The End

A time to be born, and a time to die;
Ecclesiastes 3:2 (KJV)

Chapter 13

A time to die

Everything that has a beginning has an end; to every beginning there is an end. Life has a beginning and it also has an end — in the beginning we are born and in the end we die. There is a time to be born and there is also a time to die — life doesn't just happen; it also doesn't just end.

The one thing which is certain in life, after birth, is death. As soon as a child is born the future of that child is largely unknown, unpredictable with absolute certainty and is shrouded in a lot of uncertainties; with the only predictable certainty being death. Death is about the only certainty in life; it also is its inevitable end. Death marks the end of our physical existence, just as birth signifies its commencement. And as it was in the beginning so it shall be in the end: just as the conception and exact time of delivery of each person couldn't be predicted with certainty so also cannot the exact time of a person's death be predictable with certainty. No natural birth can be predicted with absolute certainty and so also can no death, occurring naturally, be predicted with any degree of certainty.

The time of our births are not mere random coincidences but instead are specifically-timed occurrences — scheduled to occur at specific times — and for specific reasons. We are born when and how we are born for specific reasons. Similarly, the end of our natural existence doesn't come as a matter of random coincidences but, as with our births, are scheduled for specific times. Also, just as the timing of our births are carefully designed for specific reasons the time of our deaths are equally carefully designed for specific reasons. We are born at an exact time or period (e.g. day, time, year and generation) for specific reasons — almost all of which are connected to our overall purposes in life (the why we are born) — the duration of our lives have also been already determined by the one who made our existence possible (God); and the timing and manner of the end of our natural existence also are for specific reasons — possibly also connected to our overall purposes in life. We don't just die, we die for a reason.

We don't just die simply because we have to die — or else we all would have the same lifespan, dying at the same age and possibly under the same circumstances — but we die because it is time for us to die. We die because our allotted time is up. We die because our natural life has come to its end. Each life is designed in a unique way and for a unique purpose; an aspect of that uniqueness is the duration of each life. Every life has its own duration — hence people die at different stages of their respective lives, under many different circumstances. It might be worthwhile noting that there is an appointed time of death for every one of us, and that once that time is reached death is almost inevitable. I would suppose that the timing of our deaths coincide with our purposes: once the purpose of a particular life has been fulfilled, or is supposed to have been fulfilled, then such a life would naturally come to an end. This could mean that whether or not we are able to fulfil our purposes, when the appointed time of death is reached we simply have to go. Which tends to further suggest that it is possible for us to complete our natural existence without fulfilling the reasons we are born. I wouldn't imagine it is likely that our lives could be prolonged or extended simply and only because we are yet to accomplish some aspects of our overall purposes — I would imagine instead that once our time is up then it is up.

And so there is indeed a time to die; just as there also is a time to be born.

By dying we fulfil specific purposes, which with some people might easily be obvious or clearly identifiable while with some other people this purpose might be rather obscure or not easily identifiable. In some clearly identifiable cases for instance, some people might have had to die at the exact time and way they did in order to make certain things possible which could greatly benefit a particular community or groups of communities. For example, someone's death could result in a certain law being repealed, changed or modified, or replaced with a new one so as to provide a more effective protection for a particular group or groups of vulnerable people in a society who have previously either been ignored, neglected or the dangers such groups are exposed to largely underestimated or even unknown. It could be that such vulnerable groups of people might have been made to suffer various abuses (including deaths) which are largely unknown to the general public, and would've suffered even more if these abuses (including some of the conditions which could've made their occurrences possible, but which were previously largely ignored) are not exposed. And so someone, or some people, might be scheduled to die at particular times or within a certain period in order to bring the plights of such people to public knowledge so that measures could be put in place for the prevention of further abuses. An example in this regard could be Sarah's Law — or the child sex offender disclosure scheme — which was launched in England and Wales, and Scotland following the murder, by a convicted paedophile, of an eight-year-old girl named Sarah. It is possible Sarah died when and how she did so that other young children would be more adequately protected from paedophiles, especially those with previous records or convictions.

In other instances, some people might have had to die at the time and in the manner they did so that certain hidden atrocities could be exposed, and so that possible future occurrences of similar atrocities could be better prevented. Some deaths might serve as a wakeup call to humanity in general and consequently, their occurrence (including timing and mode of) might've been purposed or permitted accordingly. I suppose good examples in this regard could include deaths that occurred through genocides, ethnic cleansings and the Holocaust.

Similarly, it is possible some people might have had to die under the circumstances they did so that the secret crimes of a particular vicious criminal, for example, a serial killer, would be exposed; possibly so that such a criminal might be apprehended and brought to justice, thereby bringing an end to their evil campaign while also saving other lives who might subsequently have become victims.

And yet, some people might have had to die in particular ways and at specific times in order that the causes for which they fought might subsequently succeed. For instance, some Civil Rights activists, Freedom fighters or other types of activists may have had to die in activism — in action — and at specific times either so as to bring more public awareness to their respective causes or to finally successfully accomplish those causes. Such deaths may, for instance, result in the subsequent liberation of the groups of people, on whose behalves such activists had fought, either from tyranny, unjust governance, or other injustices (e.g. various forms of discrimination, unfair treatments, marginalisation, or manipulation, exploitations or control by external powers). Or similar deaths might bring about unity amongst a previously divided and disunited people. A few examples here could include Martin Luther King Jnr (United States of America), Stephen Bantu Biko (South Africa), Jubo Jubogha aka King Jaja of Opobo (Nigeria) and Mohandas Karamchand Gandhi aka Mahatma Gandhi (India).

Some deaths might have been planned so that their timings would assist with breakthroughs in medical or other researches. The timing of some deaths could assist with perfections of different inventions, modifications of existing but inadequate inventions, or could bring about a totally new invention either through ongoing researches or new ones which could have been specifically commissioned as a result of such deaths. It could also be possible that some of such people might've served for purposes of testing or trialling new drugs, treatments or other cures which might've been unsuccessful in their case and as a result of which success would subsequently be achieved through further researches and studies. It is also possible some people might die as a result of previously undetected diseases or infections which probably had resulted in many other deaths in the past but which were unknown at those times. It is possible it is through these new deaths that such diseases or infections would become identified, consequently leading to discoveries, through various studies or researches, for their cures and preventions. Examples here could include scientific breakthroughs in various fields, like medicine, engineering, construction, nutrition, travelling, etc. which were occasioned by the death of certain people.

There are many more other examples which could help to demonstrate that our deaths — time and manner — serve other specific purposes than merely terminating our natural existence.

And then there are other deaths whose purposes might not be easily recognisable; but suffice it to say that we don't just die because we all eventually would, but because we have to, and at a specific time too.

And so, I believe all deaths (occurring naturally) are timed to occur at specific times and for particular purposes. Please note I tried to carefully qualify that it is deaths which occur naturally — unassisted in any ways — that fulfil specific purposes and for the simple reason that everything God does is done for a reason, including the timing of deaths.

Having made this clarification, let me also point out that I believe even deaths that are assisted or apparently orchestrated by humans (e.g. suicides or the so-called assisted dying) also serve their own purposes (even if possibly not the purposes originally intended by God). Simply because I believe such deaths could only be possible where God allows them, as a result of his respect for the personal choices of the people involved. If peradventure God decides to overrule our personal choices (say, for whatever reasons) then even our decision to die at particular times and in particular ways would not yield our desired or expected results — we could try but we might not succeed in terminating our lives at will.

I strongly believe that the power of life and death lies squarely and solely in the hands of the Almighty, meaning that only God decides who is born, and when; also, having been born, when we die. At least, it seems rather obvious that we didn't orchestrate our births nor did we influence our existence in any ways possible. Consequently, I believe that only God — who caused our existence — can bring it to an end. It means then that even when some deaths occur seemingly as a result of human orchestrations, such occurrences are only possible because God allowed them (even if in accordance with human designs and scheming).

(Recall I already pointed out that we have been created with a relative freedom of choice and that God, to a greater extent, respects our various expressions of this freedom of choice. And so assuming we decide we want to terminate our lives at any given time God might choose to grant us our wishes. God, however, might also choose not to grant us such wishes, as the case may be.)

To help demonstrate the latter I will make the following factual illustrations:

- Someone jumps off a very high bridge attempting suicide, but after the desperate plunge still remains unexpectedly alive. A miracle! Moments later another person also jumps from the same bridge with a similar expectation — death by suicide — and before he or she gets to the bottom is dead. What a shame!
- Someone intentionally overdoses on a particular brand of pills, or a lethal combination of pills, in a suicide attempt and dies almost instantly. Sad! Another person somewhere else also decides to terminate their life by taking an even more lethal combination of pills, he or she overdoses, expecting to die, but to his or her dismay remains alive and well to tell his or her story. Goodness!
- A certain person, possibly believing he or she can no longer cope with what they consider to be a miserable existence, loads a gun, points it to his or her head at very close range, and pulls the trigger repeatedly. Five shots later and he or she is still alive, wondering what went wrong. Blank bullets? Unbelievable! Next door, another person with similar feelings decides to load his or her own gun, which he or she points to his or her head before firing. One shot and he or she is dead. What a way to go!

It often is the case that when some of these failed suicide attempts occur people would sometimes remark that the time for the persons in question "hadn't come", implying that such persons survived their suicide attempts because it wasn't yet time for them to die — which somehow serves as an acknowledgement that there is indeed a time to die. When someone attempts to end his or her life but fails; it tends to confirm that our lives are not necessarily in our own hands and that someone else could be responsible for our lives in general including our births and deaths — God is.

And so even with deaths that could be said to have been orchestrated by humans, God is still ultimately responsible, in that he has to first permit their occurrence (as planned and timed) before they could happen accordingly. Or otherwise such deaths would not go as planned or intended.

There are also some deaths which are not necessarily suicides but could still be said to have been orchestrated by humans: some deaths could be seen as resulting from deliberate attempts or actions by human beings, possibly people other than those who died as a result of such actions. For example, murders, accidental discharge of firearms, involuntary murders, genocides, wars, ritual killings through diabolical means, etc. could all result in deaths. And then there are those other deaths, which could be regarded as occurring naturally, but which are considered so atrocious that it could be doubtful God has permitted them: some natural disasters, like landslides, earthquakes, tsunamis, storms, or other disasters, like epidemics, so-called terminal diseases, road accidents, or plane crashes could result in many deaths.

In both sets of circumstances, it is possible to wonder whether such deaths could not have been entirely controlled or influenced by their apparent respective causes without God having anything to do with them — we may wonder whether God would indeed permit the occurrence of such atrocities.

While I will not attempt advocating on behalf of God, permit me to briefly remark that God would often allow our choices even when our choices contradict his wishes and plans; he would also often allow the consequences of such choices. I already pointed out that most of the things for which we blame God could actually be due to our direct actions. For instance, we may choose to continuously landfill some parts of different oceans, seas or rivers or to excessively dredge these water bodies; with the subsequent effects of flooding, landslides or earthquakes all of which might result in mass deaths (both of humans and animals) and other costly damages. Or we may fail to properly protect or take care of our ecosystems, either due to mass deforestations, decimation of particular animal or plant populations, or other unhealthy activities like dumping of toxic substances at wrong places; with the resultant effects of diseases and epidemics which might result in mass deaths. Or some parts of the world, or particular groups in a given region, might subject other parts of the world, or other groups in the same region, to one or more forms of abuses, exploitations, or oppressions which might culminate in one or more forms of violence, for example, wars, insurgencies, guerrilla warfare, or other acts which could result in mass deaths. In these instances, and many others, the deaths occurring are direct or indirect consequences of our choices including our actions and inactions; it is possible God might've chosen to respect our choices and in so doing has also allowed that we face the consequences of both our choices and actions possibly as deterrents to encourage or help us make better choices subsequently, or take corrective measures to remedy previous wrong choices made as well as their consequences.

The bottom line, however, is that God is ultimately responsible for life and death — regardless of their real or apparent and direct or indirect causes. Generally-speaking, things happen either because they were ordained by God to happen or because, though not necessarily intended by him, God allowed them to happen as a result of his respect for the choices made by humans.

To help demonstrate that even these other deaths — due to natural disasters and general human activities or direct individual actions — are all still under God's control I will make the following illustrations:

- Someone, having been diagnosed with a so-called terminal disease is told he or she can only remain alive for a maximum of six months only meaning that, going by medical prognosis, he or she is expected to be dead within six months; he or she, however, goes on to live for another thirty years before dying, not as a result of

the disease whose symptoms are still very much present in his or her body, but of other unrelated causes. Another person, having also been diagnosed with the same disease, but whose prognosis suggests he or she has a very good chance of surviving for about ten more years dies within a few months of the initial diagnosis.
- There is a ghastly plane crash from which there are no expected human survivors; almost every passenger die but a lone survivor is later found somewhere in the bushes almost unscathed except for some minor injuries.
- A building collapses leaving many people dead as a result, about five days later a child is found alive and rescued from the debris while under the same debris and in the same location as the child many adults and other children are found dead.
- An assassination attempt is made on the life of a person during which he or she was shot multiply and later left for dead; they, however, survive the gunshots and remain alive. In another instance, a single stray bullet hits an unintended victim killing him or her instantly.
- A person is poisoned over an extended period of time with a particular poisonous substance, in amounts which ordinarily should kill them; they remain alive, totally oblivious of the fact he or she had been subjected to a poisonous substance, subsequently leaving his or her intended-killer puzzled and maybe even leading to a confession from him or her. Another person unintentionally ingests a smaller amount of the same poisonous substance and dies almost immediately.
- Someone, unbeknown to him or her, is subjected to a series of diabolical attacks, intended to kill him or her, but the attacks are unsuccessful leading to confessions from his or her intended-killer. Meanwhile, similar diabolical rituals by the same perpetrator results in the death of another victim.
- A young soldier goes on his or her first tour of duty, is shot and dies. His or her comrade, also shot in the same tour of duty, survives; and later also survives many more tours of duty until he or she is retired at old age.

I suppose these few examples tend to imply that death doesn't necessarily occur simply because we are exposed to circumstances or situations which could kill; it tends to prove that death occurs only when God allows it. If those circumstances alone could kill then they would always result in death, but the simple fact that they do not always result in death suggests that though they could result in death they do not have the absolute power to kill: they are only effective as instruments of death when God permits that death should occur and to occur through them.

With respect to the timing of individual deaths therefore, it is reasonable to conclude that there is a set time for each death to occur — a time to die — and God is responsible for that timing.

Consequently, since there is a time to die, since we do not control that timing nor can independently influence it in any way, and because we do not know with any degree of certainty when death may occur it becomes a necessity that we endeavour to live circumspectly.

> So teach us to number our days, that we may apply our hearts unto wisdom. (Psalms 90:12;KJV)

In addition to the above reference there is also a popular contemporary slogan which poignantly captures life: YOLO — an acronym for You Only Live Once. YOLO, in my opinion, pensively but aptly reminds us of both the limited and terminal nature of our natural lives. It seems to suggest that since we have only one life we have to make the most of it.

The sad irony, however, is that this ingenious invention — YOLO — is often misapplied by some people such that it seems that they use it as a type of justification or even motivation to encourage living recklessly or to indulge in daring, dangerous or damaging activities. Some people seem to use YOLO as a reason to do whatever they please seemingly unconcerned about the consequences of such actions. A rather disturbing, perplexing and pitiable situation which is both bereft of sensibility and also defies sound reasoning because when we know we have only one life each then we would rather be expected to be more careful with how we live our lives instead of living it anyhow that tickles our fancies at any given moment.

When we know we have only one shot at something we often exercise due diligence before and while taking our aim, so as to ensure we are successful at our first and only attempt since there are no second chances. For instance, a person sitting for an examination for which there are no second chances would not likely go into that examination unprepared; he or she would not likely treat the actual examination with contempt, recklessness or levity but would instead likely do everything within his or her powers to ensure success in that only attempt available for passing the examination: He or she is very likely to study very hard in advance of the examination including practising and revising with previous examination papers where applicable and he or she would likely try to ensure that he or she arrives at the exam venue on time with sufficient time for settling down and getting ready for the exam proper; he or she is most likely to try and do everything required to pass the exam in that one and only chance.

Similarly, a person attending a job interview where there are no second chances would more likely try to do everything required for a success in that interview: He or she is likely to be appropriately dressed for the interview, would arrive early, would be polite and professional, and wouldn't be uncouth; he or she would also try to answer questions as correctly and carefully as he or she best can; and he or she would do everything possible which would guarantee success in the interview.

In each of these instances, the persons involved would ordinarily be expected to do some degree of planning, preparation and reviewing and to also actually implement such plans, having been made, otherwise they risk failing instead of succeeding — which could mean a wasted opportunity. It means then that YOLO should actually encourage us to be more circumspect with how we choose to live our lives, and not be an excuse to live recklessly or irresponsibly. It tends to suggest that we should treat our lives with respect exercising due diligence at all times so as to ensure we live fulfilled and satisfied lives: Which might require us to do some advance planning in preparing for life's various stages and circumstances while also having regular reviews of our past actions to assess either their profitability or propriety and, more importantly, living in ways which ensure that we leave behind lasting legacies, which might include having helped and touched the lives of our contemporaries in one or more positive ways as well as leaving things which would be beneficial to future generations.

But reality seems to suggest that although we all know we would die someday, some people (probably in the majority) live as though our natural lives will continue forever — some people live as though they will live for ever. Otherwise, if we truly acknowledge we would die someday, we are more likely to live differently doing many things differently.

How might we live differently?

First, and foremost, let us try to identify that thing which almost every one of us aspire and strive for, which practically fuels our drive and ambition, and for which everybody labour; which also, as a matter of fact, everyone require for the daily satisfaction of their needs without which living might become almost impossible. And what might that be?

Money.

There is no gainsaying the fact that we all need money — or broadly-speaking, wealth or economic resources with which we provide for our needs — or else how would we be able to meet our daily needs. I guess this might be why money is regarded by some as all-important and a must-have. That we all need money in order to provide for our daily and other needs, however, does not necessarily imply that we have to be driven or controlled by it.

Money, without a doubt, is a vital necessity in life; having sufficient money, enough to cater for our needs, is also another vital life necessity. Seeking after money the right way is also another vital life necessity because overindulgence in this venture could greatly undermine the quality of our lives.

Incidentally, it is in our pursuit of money that some of us have gone awfully wrong so that instead of being driven by our needs we have become driven by the mere desire to have lots and lots of money or wealth. Consequently, in our desperation, it seems we often ignore our true needs while pursuing other vain desires which offer no real satisfaction. More so, some people strive so hard to accumulate wealth in abundance and end up accumulating more wealth than they need which often results in very reasonable proportions of such wealth ultimately becoming useless and worthless to the people who have accumulated them — when we die we leave the world empty-handed meaning that whatever is left behind is of no use to us. YOLO means we couldn't return to life a second time to take advantage of the excess wealth we might've left behind; since people don't usually accumulate wealth just so as to leave surpluses after they die, it would then mean whatever is left behind after a person dies is effectively useless to him or her even if other people would later benefit from such wealth.

It means such endeavours might be rightly regarded as vain or fruitless endeavours — vanity! —— which, incidentally, is how one of the world's richest and apparently wisest kings — King Solomon — sees it:

> Vanity of vanities, saith the Preacher, vanity of vanities; all is vanity.
> What profit hath a man of all his labour which he taketh under the sun?
> One generation passeth away, and another generation cometh: but the earth abideth for ever.
> (Ecclesiastes 1:2 – 4;KJV)

And also:

> All things are full of labour; man cannot utter it: the eye is not satisfied with seeing, nor the ear filled with hearing. (Ecclesiastes 1:8;KJV)

And:

> I have seen all the works that are done under the sun; and, behold, all is vanity and vexation of spirit. (Ecclesiastes 1:14;KJV)

Considering that the person who made the above statements is the same person who made an earlier statement, referenced previously: "Money answereth all things", these statements each now becomes more significant and acquires a deeper meaning. Why would King Solomon, who earlier said: money answereth all things, later say: all — including money — is vanity? I wonder.

However, when someone who's supposed to have been there and done that speaks I guess those who are merely aspiring to "be there" and to "do that" ought to listen, and to listen very attentively with a view not only of comprehending but also of putting into useful application whatever it is that is being said.

But why would a man, who apparently had it all, suddenly sound melancholic? Why would the richest king of his time say: everything that man does under the sun is meaningless, futile and a trouble to the spirit? Or why would King Solomon even question the profitability of human endeavours? Whereas in our days, when most people, who are deemed successful, are asked the secret behind their success would often attribute it to working very hard: "Work, work and more work", they would often say implying that hard work is the secret to success. If working hard, however, is truly the secret of success why then would a wise and rich king regard it as unfruitful and a vexation of the human spirit? Experience, they say, is the best teacher and I believe that King Solomon is speaking from a personal and direct experience; we all know that lessons earned from an experience could never be overemphasised nor could they be undermined. Also, seeing that it is better to gain from someone else's experiences instead of having to earn them ourselves, by having to undergo similar experiences, I would suppose then that we could greatly benefit from the wisdom and personal experiences of the wise King Solomon, which would be much better than having to earn such wisdom from our own direct and personal experiences which might come at great personal costs.

- And so one of the primary (and possibly most important) thing we could do differently would be to reassess the degree of importance we attach to money; which in turn should lead us to change how we pursue it.

Presently, going by what popularly obtains today, it would seem that more people seem to be trying to provide eternal solutions for temporal problems — our natural needs — because some of us ignorantly seek to accumulate wealth as though making provisions which would last forever, whereas in fact, even the world itself will not last for ever. Conversely, it would also seem that most of us only pay a cursory attention to our eternal need — our soul — because some of us tend to assume or behave as though the soul would expire once the body dies (actually, more like the soul dies while the body lives for ever), whereas that isn't true as our souls, as a matter of fact, are eternal as well as immortal while our bodies are temporal and mortal. We seem to have gotten it all wrong and mixed-up.

As a result, we desperately need to reset our priorities getting them in their right order if we are to learn from some of the wisdom of King Solomon and if we are to spare ourselves of disappointment at the end of our natural lives. To be able to do this, however, we need wisdom which, incidentally, seems to be a position also supported by the wise King Solomon:

> Wisdom is the principal thing; therefore get wisdom: and with all thy getting get understanding. (Proverbs 4:7;KJV)

It is instructive to note that he says: "with all thy getting", meaning with all your accumulations, possessions and assets make sure to also accumulate and possess wisdom ensuring it is part of your assets. Or as you strive, or (as the rich people of our time will tell us) as you work, work, and more work make sure to also strive or work, work and more work to acquire the asset or estate of wisdom and understanding. Wisdom, he seems to be suggesting, is not only vital but is also very valuable.

And why wisdom?

According to an old English proverb:

> "A fool & his money,
> be soon at debate:
> which after with sorrow,
> repents him too late."
>
> (Thomas Tusser; Five Hundreth Pointes of Good Husbandrie, 1573)

Which was later precisely worded:

"A fool and his money is soon parted."

In the absence of wisdom, we could risk losing everything we have laboured so hard to acquire. However, the risk of losing our wealth isn't the primary or only reason we are encouraged to get wisdom and it shouldn't be our main motivation for seeking wisdom because, more than merely helping us secure our wealth, wisdom is a vital necessity in life; it is the founding and guiding pillar of life without which life would not only be meaningless but also almost impossible. We need wisdom for practically everything we do in life including living life itself or else we risk living badly or wrongly.

Wisdom, however, is not the same thing as knowledge or intelligence: Knowledge is the possession of information or skills; intelligence is the propensity or ability to acquire information or skills — knowledge — while wisdom is the application of the knowledge which has been acquired. Merely possessing a lot of information or skills — knowledge — or having a naturally high propensity or aptitude for the acquisition of information or skills — intelligence — is of little or no benefit where and when such information or skills are not put into their right use or application. Applying the knowledge in our possession for their right use is only what makes such knowledge relevant and beneficial, otherwise such knowledge is practically useless. And so wisdom is more important than knowledge and intelligence; it is also more relevant because it is wisdom which gives both relevance and benefit to knowledge and intelligence.

If, for instance, someone has a car but continues to do every of his or her commuting by public transport and on foot, I wouldn't suppose that car could be considered as being of any tangible benefit to its owner. It would just be a mere property which has no real utility — pointless! A car is only useful when used for commuting; knowledge also is only useful when applied. Wisdom is that application.

It then means that for us to be rightly considered as wise we must put into their right use every knowledge in our possession. It means then that if we are truly wise we would begin to now apply everything we have learnt so far as a result of the journey — the journey of life. For instance, knowing that someday we would die and that it could happen at any time, for which we do not know when — knowledge — if we are wise then we would put that knowledge into good use and we would live as people who know they would die and could die at anytime when exactly they do not know — wisdom. Does that then suggest having to live everyday with the fear of death looming over us? Absolutely not! As a matter of fact, if we live as people who truly acknowledge the certainty of death and the uncertainty of its timing, we would conduct our lives in ways that death or the thought of death would hold no terror or frightful prospect to us: if we live as though we would die someday, any day, then we would not be afraid of dying because we would then live in ways which would mean that we are ready for death anytime it comes calling. Similarly, we would concern ourselves primarily with those things which are really important and absolutely necessary for our existence which I suppose are also the things we need for the fulfilment of our purposes — the reason we are here in the first place.

Another thing we could do differently as a result of having become wise, could be in getting not all that we can but only all that we need: Doing that would guarantee that we avoid all the negative and damaging consequences of greed and the excessive accumulation of wealth, and also, the attendant unhealthy and exerting efforts required for such accumulations — it would free us of every avoidable stress and fruitless endeavours; a relatively stress-free living would almost definitely result in a happier, more satisfying and fulfilling life.

One more thing we could do differently through wisdom could be endeavouring to know our true self, acknowledging and respecting our uniqueness and living the life we really like to live: It may lead us to try discovering our talents, skills or abilities and our deciding to exploit them to their full potentials instead of trying to aspire for those things for which we have no natural abilities. We might, for instance, discover we are talented technically and so pursue technical vocations instead of pursuing academic careers, simply because possessing a university degree seems to be more respected in our societies, even though we are not naturally academically brilliant. Going contrary to our natural grains, by insisting on obtaining a university degree, for instance, when we know we are not brilliant academically, could mean that we struggle relatively harder to get through a university education; and even after obtaining a university degree, we might also discover we have no genuine interests in putting our university degrees to their right use and for the relevant jobs.

Getting to know our true selves could also make us aware of what our real needs are so that instead of aspiring to accumulate so much wealth we may simply attend to our needs thereby protecting ourselves from avoidable stress and strife. We may also discover our true passions, which in turn could lead us to do only the things we really like to do and need to do and not the things which other people are doing; and to do the things which we not only enjoy doing but which could also enrich our lives, and those of others, in many ways.

All-in-all, getting to know our true selves would enable us to live in sync with God's designs for our lives, which in turn would ensure that we live almost effortlessly.

I suppose there are many things we could do differently, but suffice it to say that if we do daily everything we could possibly do, in the best ways we possibly could living one day at a time and doing only what is required in order to take care of our needs as and when they arise without unduly stressing over a tomorrow we are not even sure of, without trying to own the whole world then we possibly should have lived as best we could. We would then have no regrets because we would've assured ourselves that we have done everything we could, when we could and how best we could — what more could we do?

Fortunately, I don't suppose God expects more from us: if we have done as much as our maker wanted us to do (or at least our bests) then we would look upon returning to him positively and with excitement. Again, we wouldn't be afraid of death or of dying.

It means then that if we live well we would also die well; If we live right we would also die right. Conversely, if we live badly we would die badly; if we live wrongly we would die wrongly. It is only when we live badly or wrongly that death becomes a frightful and an undesirable prospect.

Whichever be the case, we must remember there is a time to die.

Chapter 14

Goodbye, World

Death is about the most unwelcome and unsavoury subject of discussion among humans; yet, it is the one thing which is unavoidable in life and that would befall every human. Considering its certainty and inevitability, it rather would've been expected that we would find the subject of death (and dying) an interesting even if not altogether exciting one. As it so happens, however, most people prefer to avoid any discussion bordering on death. It is as though we believe we would be inviting our death, prematurely, were we to constantly discuss about death; and that if we carefully avoided any discussion about death, we might then somehow be able to keep death away, at least as long as possible.

Consequently, in some older cultures, death was even considered a taboo while referring to it directly or explicitly as death was forbidden and almost inconceivable; so instead, death was referred to in many indirect ways but not directly as death. Similarly, in most modern cultures even, as if to minimise the impact of death, people often prefer to refer to it in many indirect ways, using various euphemisms, instead of referring to it as death or to die. For instance, we might say someone has crossed to the great beyond or to the other side, passed on, given up the ghost, is no more or no longer with us, or that he or she has transited instead of simply saying that such a person had died. It would seem as though we feel more comfortable referring to death using euphemisms than referring to it directly as death.

Similarly, people, expectedly, behave and conduct themselves differently when around a dead or dying person: we often treat such cases with a certain degree of reverence, decorum and solemnity. For instance, it is generally deemed more appropriate that people are quiet and behave soberly at funeral services, or when visiting gravesides at cemeteries; they are also expected to behave solemnly during such circumstances. Attitudes, I suppose, which smack more of respect for death than for its victims — as it seems that we actually are paying respect to death through its victims.

Consequently, it would seem as though we accord more respect to death than to life, and to dying than to living. Ironically, however, death is actually an integral part of life, and, relatively, a very tiny aspect of life even because it simply brings the natural aspect of life to its end — death is the short end of a long story. And so, we actually are supposed to respect life as much as we respect its natural end death — (maybe respect it more than death even).

While I am not absolutely certain our behaviours and attitudes towards death could be considered rational, they obviously appear cautious as it seems, by avoiding talking about death or by according it so much respect, we hope to somehow keep it at bay for as long as possible (even if we couldn't avoid or escape it completely). But we ought to know that isn't the case, since whether or not we choose to talk about death, or we treat it with so much or so little respect our decisions do not and could not make any difference since we will all eventually die.

And so, why then do we treat death the way we do: with so much respect, and sometimes with what could be described as fear? Why do we prefer not to talk about it? Why do we prefer to keep it, in a manner of speaking, locked in a closet? Why do we often shy away from talking about death? Why is it some people behave in ways which tend to suggest they wished we didn't have to die? Why do most people act as though they are in awe of death?

I suppose the main reason for our seemingly reverential attitude towards death might be simple and obvious: death is the one thing for which we have no cure, which we couldn't avoid and which is totally outside our control or influence. Death is beyond us, as it were, and as a result we wrongly assume that it is more powerful than us, with the result that we prefer to avoid it as much as is possible. It is possible it is because death is totally outside our control that we prefer to keep our distance from anything to do with it. It is also possible it is for this reason that we behave as if we are afraid of death. It might also be that our seeming respect or reverence of death is driven by this apparent helplessness we feel with respect to death.

Although death might be beyond our control, is inevitable and has no cure, is death, however, truly powerful? Or is death even more powerful than us? Are we all at death's mercy? Can death simply, arbitrarily, swoop down and pluck any one of us it wants to? Is death looming over us, waiting to pounce any time it pleases?

Are we afraid of death? Should we be?

To help us correctly answer these questions, we must first understand what death truly is. By properly understanding what death is we are more likely to correctly comprehend what it can and cannot do.

What is death?

First, and foremost, we must recognise that death is not an independent entity per se — it hasn't got its own will: death does not exist as a free enterprise, able to freely operate independently without any forms of control. Death, as a matter of fact, is merely a messenger — somewhat similar to money which is just a means to an end but which on its own is worthless (in the case of death, powerless) — who becomes relevant only when there are messages to be delivered. In the absence of messages, a messenger remains dormant: the postman or post woman wouldn't be knocking on a door for which he or she hasn't got letters or deliveries — messages — for.

Life

And so we shall regard death as a type of postman or post woman — messenger: You wouldn't normally be afraid of your local postman or post woman now, would you?

Death is a spirit; one of God's many spirit-messengers. It couldn't operate arbitrarily or independently but is always under God's control, instructions and guidance. It is only when death is sent on an errand, by the Almighty, that it comes alive and is activated otherwise it remains dormant and in a dormant state. It means then death couldn't arbitrarily swoop low and grab any one of us if and when God Almighty has not instructed it to do so. And so, in the absence of God's will and authorisation, death could be said to be dead, quite literally.

Similarly, it means that when death is "not in service" — when it hasn't been sent by God on a mission — it is powerless. If death cannot act at will (actually, has no will of its own), it simply means it couldn't do anything unless and until empowered by God. And so death could be likened to a grim monster whose powers are not intrinsic but are vested upon it, as and when required, and are entirely outside its own control. Death is a grim monster who until empowered, through divine instruction, is entirely powerless and harmless. It means then this grim monster could only overwhelm us when it has been empowered to do so by our maker — God. Otherwise, as grim as this monster might be, it is absolutely of no threat to us.

And so, should we fear death?

To help the question, I will propose as follows: Should you fear a messenger who couldn't knock on your door except he or she has a message for you? Should you fear a monster which couldn't on its own harm you? Should you fear someone who doesn't even know that you exist, except when informed accordingly; and who would only be informed about your existence when you have lived your life to its full?

Death is very much like a ferry service — which only helps us cross to the other side: You don't need the services of a ferry except you have to cross from one side to another side. More so, you only get on board a ferry when you've come to cross to the other side or else you wouldn't be there in the first place. Ferries don't come to us, we go to them: likewise, death doesn't come to us we go to meet it. Each day of our lives spent is a step closer to our death, we continue marching forward and, finally, we approach death only when we have come to the end of our natural lives and it is time for us to die. But death wouldn't and couldn't meet us midway in our journey, and couldn't meet us until and except we approach it as our journey comes to its natural end. Similarly, death wouldn't and couldn't ferry us across to the great beyond unless and until it time for us to transit and we have found ourselves at the ferry crossing needing death's ferry service.

The last chapter intimated us that there is a time to die, now we shall look at why we die.

Why do we die?

Some people wrongly assume that death is a punishment, that when death comes it is only because we have done something terribly wrong or have accumulated so much wrong deeds through persistently doing wrong. I would suppose that might be why we sometimes refer to death as "the Grim Reaper", possibly implying that it comes to mete out rewards or to harvest our souls when we have sown enough wild oats. But we should know that isn't true because everyone — good people, bad people and all people — die. (Ironically, contrary to this presumption, oftentimes some people who might've lived wickedly or atrociously outlive their well-behaved and goodly counterparts.) Consequently, since we all die, it would be wrong to presume that death is a punishment.

We die simply because our natural existence has been limited by the Creator:

> And the Lord God said, Behold, the man is become as one of us, to know good and evil: and now, lest he put forth his hand, and take also of the tree of life, and eat, and live for ever:

> Therefore the Lord God sent him forth from the garden of Eden, to till the ground from whence he was taken.
> (Genesis 3:22,23;KJV)

Please note that our spirits cannot die — because they are products of the immortal breath of life from God — and so the living for ever, in reference here, is of our physical bodies or our natural lives. We cannot live for ever in our physical bodies because God prevented that from being a possibility, by sending Adam and Eve away from the garden of Eden so that they couldn't eat of the tree of life, which would've made them physically immortal. Our spirits however, are, and remain, immortal.

The death of the spirit, which would've been necessitated as a consequence for the wilful transgression of Adam and Eve, was graciously averted through the atonement made on this behalf by the Lord God. Consequently, the immortality of the human spirit is retained and sustained.

Since God is responsible for the entirety of our existence, it is only reasonable to conclude that he is also responsible for its end — death. And so we die because God has made it so.

We have so far been intimated that there is a time to die and that we die because God made us so; we shall now reflect on when we die.

When do we die?

It might be worth reiterating now that discussing death or spending some time reflecting about it wouldn't somehow accelerate the time of death. On the contrary, spending a little time to try to understand death might actually help us to live better lives. On the issue of when we die, I already remarked at the beginning of the last chapter that the time of death (as the time of birth) cannot be accurately predicted with absolute certainty. Consequently, it would simply suffice to say that we couldn't know exactly when it is time for us to die except God informs us accordingly.

Do you, however, really want to know when you will die? And how might that information help you? I personally think that such information might be more unhelpful than helpful as it might expose us to avoidable stress and distress. Imagine living through life knowing exactly when you will die. Pressure?

I am personally grateful to God that he chose to spare us with such information or knowledge and that he often intimates some people with this information only when it would be very useful for them and when they are emotionally matured, prepared and ready to handle the weight of such knowledge.

I am sufficed with the knowledge that I will die only when it is time for me to die — a time chosen by my creator, God — and that I couldn't die until it is that time. It might suffice you too.

I suppose a better and truer understanding of the truths surrounding death is an important necessity in life, as I believe we could live better if we understood death better. In trying to understand death we are more likely to also understand life better — the true meaning of death would reveal the true meaning of life because the former is only the end of the latter. For instance, understanding that death is the end of our natural journeys should help us to better appreciate the finiteness and brevity of the journey itself. Consequently, we might better appreciate life aspiring to make the most of it. It might mean our endeavouring to enjoy everything life presents us — whether considered good or bad — because we might then understand that whatever circumstances we encounter are only transient and couldn't last forever, meaning that a better attitude could be to make the most of everything life offers since none will last forever. We might then endeavour to take advantage of everything we encounter.

Similarly, understanding that life is a journey and that past and present encounters could prepare us to better tackle possible future encounters could mean that we do our best in learning from our experiences and circumstances. It might mean endeavouring to learn the lessons inherent in our circumstances since almost every situations we find ourselves in have something beneficial for us in them. For instance, something which might initially or presently appear irrelevant or a setback might actually be helpful in preparing us for something ahead which could be better and bigger, or it might even be the avenue through which we would be transported to something wonderful. (How many times have we looked back at circumstances, which at the time of their occurrence seemed meaningless, or might've caused us so much suffering and grief, only to later appreciate them because they turned out to be beneficial to us in ways we never could've expected or imagined? Or how many times have we looked upon past experiences with nostalgia and longing, experiences which at the time we desperately wished away or wanted to be over as quick as possible? We often refer to the "good old days" but the irony is that most times in those days we saw nothing good in them.)

Similarly, understanding that life is a one-way journey — journey of no return — might mean that we would exercise due diligence by doing everything that we are opportune to do whenever the opportunity arises to do them so that we are at no time left with unfinished businesses especially when we could easily have finished such businesses at other times. It could mean that since we know death could strike at any time we live in ways which would mean that we are not caught napping or unawares. It might lead us to becoming very cautious with procrastination meaning that we might begin to live in the now: doing whatever could be done at any given time that very given time, and not having to postpone doing it hoping for a more convenient time in the future.

> Whatsoever thy hand findeth to do, do it with thy might; for there is no work, nor device, nor knowledge, nor wisdom, in the grave, whither thou goest. (Ecclesiastes 9:10;KJV)

Also, understanding that life has no return tickets might encourage us to endeavour getting most things right, and to live rightly since after death there would be no second chances during which we might be able to make restitutions or reparations for wrongs. After death, we are not able to return back to life to put things right even if we would want to.

It might lead us to try to always be true to our innermost convictions and passions at all times and not to be easily swayed by popular cultures or peer or societal pressures or expectations. Furthermore, it might encourage us to ensure we have the right convictions — founded on truths.

Also, understanding that in death we are bereft of every earthly possessions might encourage us to be more contented with the things we have and to enjoy them while we still can. It might also help us to become less self-centred and more selfless. We could learn to become more charitable. (One of life's many ironies is that it is in giving that we receive more, so that the more we give away is the more that is returned to us. But, unfortunately, it would seem those who want to have more refuse to share what they already have wrongly believing that if they gave away anything they would be left short. The truth, however, is it is by giving that our resources are increased. Similarly, the biggest beneficiaries of any acts of kindness or charity are the people doing them and not the people to whom they are done. The satisfaction derivable from giving (i.e. when it is done for the right reasons, in the right ways, and not with ulterior motives) is better and more experienced by a giver than a receiver as the joy of seeing someone else satisfied or observing his or her life change positively as a result of our kind efforts is simply priceless. But, again, we often wrongly assume that the people who receive assistance from others are the primary and only beneficiaries of such kind gestures.)

It might also mean that we would refuse to clamour or to accumulate more that we need, meaning that we could live better lives free of avoidable stress.

It might also mean that instead of trying to outdo one another in ostentation we would focus on acquiring only those things we truly need. More so, it could also mean that we would endeavour to acquire only those things we could really benefit from and which we really like, and not to acquire things mainly because they are in popular demand and more people acquire them.

Similarly, understanding that once we die our mortal existence comes to an end, so that whatever happens afterwards are in no way relevant to us and do not affect or impact us in anyways, might help us to concern ourselves primarily with our own mortal existence meaning that we wouldn't bother ourselves during our lifetime with what might or might not happen after we die.

For instance, some people worry endlessly about perpetuating their existence (or that of their ancestry), by seeking to ensure that their lineage continues after they are gone. And so they may strongly desire to have at least one offspring, especially a male one since it is generally believed that lineages can only be continued through male children, and as a result such people may be willing to practically do anything they can in their bid to have a child including marrying more than a wife or having multiple concubines or mistresses, thereby consequently desecrating the sanctity of holy matrimony and falling foul of the will and instructions of God Almighty. Some others, who already have been blessed with only female children, sometimes behave similarly in search of a male child. And yet some others end up having more children (boys and girls), which, in some cases, could be more than they can adequately provide for, just so as to ensure that in the event any of those children die prematurely there would still be other children left to carry on with their lineage (as if by having many children they are guaranteed that at least one of those children would definitely survive them).

Consequently, many marriages have either been terminated abruptly, destroyed or rendered unenjoyable or unsatisfying simply because they lacked children or a child took long to arrive, or because they lacked male children. By behaving in those or similar ways, such people seem to ignore the fact that we are not responsible for our existence; our existence derive from God's grand plans meaning that it is up to him whose and what lineages are continued or perpetuated, it is also up to God who has what children. They also seem to forget that multiple marriages could not guarantee childbirth or particular sexes of children.

These facts aside, however, would it really matter to us when our natural lives are ended whether or not we have children? Does anything that takes place after we are dead have any real impacts upon our entire existence? Does having a continuing lineage somehow benefit us after death?

It might just be an illusion that our lives are continued through our children. Once we die our natural existence ends: The dead do not know what happens after they are gone; whether they have children, what becomes of such children, whether those children go on to have children of their own, what becomes of such children of children, whether such children of children subsequently go on to have their own children and what becomes of such third-tier children and so on and so forth. And so it is possible that lineage is only relevant to the living not the dead. The dead have no business whatsoever in the land of the living and though those who are still alive might wish to remember those who have died, and so might try to keep the memories of the dead alive in many different ways (e.g. monuments, foundations, naming subsequent births after dead relatives, etc.), the truth is that the dead do not know (nor do they care) whether or not they are remembered or how they are remembered.

Life, and living, and everything connected to both are only relevant to those who are alive; the dead, regardless of their statuses in life (e.g. parent or no parent, rich or poor, famous or unknown, great or small, etc.), all share a common and same status — they all become spirits, which are unaffected in any ways by their previous natural lifetime statuses.

As a result of this misconception — that we could still somehow influence life after we are dead or that whatever happens after our death might still be somehow relevant to us — some people also strive to make provisions for their posterities. Consequently, some people apply a reasonable proportion of their natural existence in trying to accumulate as much wealth as possible, so that when they eventually die they could leave behind enough wealth for those that they leave behind them, but the fact is that when such people die they have no way of knowing what really become of the wealth that they leave behind; whether or not their respective posterities are eventually able to retain such wealth or whether or not such wealth are well managed by such posterities.

There are instances where a person's ill-gotten wealth and assets, for instance, have either been frozen or confiscated by a constituted authority like governments, or where some people's estates would later become subjects of litigations, following their death, such that the chances of the posterities of such people successfully inheriting the estates bequeathed to them couldn't be guaranteed. Similarly, in other cases, the value of a deceased estates might later depreciate in value, after his or her death, losing a lot of value due to market conditions or all of its value for one reason or another with the result that such estates, unbeknownst to the dead, are no longer as valuable as they were during the deceased's lifetime; consequently the estates may fail to accomplish the desires of the individual leaving them behind and their intended purpose, that of helping to provide for the needs of their beneficiaries. As a result, the desires and aspirations of such individuals in wanting to provide for their posterity could very easily be undermined in any of many different ways, none of which such dead people could do absolutely anything about, so that all their well-meaning endeavours, in accumulating excessive wealth for their posterity, could end up becoming futile.

Which simply emphasises the very limited nature of our powers and abilities, which in turn highlights the truth that life as a whole is under the direct and sole control of the creator — the almighty God — and as we often say "man proposes but God disposes". This seems to suggest that it would be more sensible committing our desires to God, since only him can bring them to pass, instead of trying to accomplish them by our own efforts.

Finally, understanding that death is a passage between here and the hereafter or between mortality and immortality — a transition — could mean that instead of focusing all of our attention and efforts on this side of live alone we might invest some of our attention and efforts towards preparing ourselves for the other side of life.

Similarly, realising that once we die the present world ceases to be of any significance to us, we couldn't alter or amend the things we have done therein and we couldn't in any ways influence anything which goes on in it we are likely to consider more what might lie ahead after death than to concern ourselves with what might happen in the world we would be leaving behind after we are gone. If we realise that when our mortal lives end our immortality begin, we would make some efforts to ensure that our immortal existence would be better than our mortal existence especially since the former far outweighs the latter.

Seeing then that acquainting ourselves with death — what it is — could do us some good, it might be worthwhile changing our present culture of avoiding, as much as we possibly could, pondering it. So that instead of avoiding pondering death we might rather embrace it — in trying to understand it — so that we could better understand what it really is; we might then be able to come to terms with the idea of dying since in trying to better understand death we would most definitely understand life better. Understanding life better would encourage us to make the most of it including ensuring that before we say goodbye to the world we are well prepared to welcome a glorious eternity.

To end the chapter I will leave you with few "last words" of different people who lived here before but now have bade the world farewell. These quotations have been randomly selected and for no particular reasons other than that they help to convey the message: someday we too will bid the world farewell we would be saying, "Goodbye, World."

- "Don't die like I did." (George Best; 1946 –2005; a footballer)
- "Adieu, mes amis. Je vais `a la gloire." : "Farewell, my friends. I go to glory" (Isadora Duncan;1878 –1927; a dancer)
- "This is it. I'm going. I'm going." (Al Jolson; 1886 – 1950)
- "Die, my dear Doctor, that's the last thing I shall do!" (Lord Henry Temple Palmerston; 1784 –1865; a former Prime Minister)
- "Let me go to the house of the Father." (Pope John Paul II; 1920 – 2005; a former Pope)

Life

- "So little done, so much to do." (Cecil Rhodes; 1853 - 1902; a politician)
- "Lord take my soul, but the struggle continues." (Ken Saro-Wiwa; 1941 - 1995; a writer and environmental activist)
- "See in what peace a Christian can die." (Joseph Addison; 1672 -1719; an essayist, poet, playwright and politician)
- "Oh God, here I go." (Max Baer; 1909 -1959; a boxing Heavyweight Champion)
- "I can't sleep." (James Barrie; 1860 - 1937; an author)
- "Now comes the mystery." (Henry Ward Beecher; 1813 - 1887; a clergyman, social reformer and speaker)
- "Standing, as I do, in view of God and eternity I realise that patriotism is not enough. I must have no hatred or bitterness towards anyone." (Edith Louisa Cavell; 1865 -1915; a nurse)
- "Goodbye, Everybody!" (Hart Crane; 1899 - 1932; a poet)
- "I die happy." (Charles James Fox; 1749 - 1806; a politician)
- "Why are you weeping? Did you imagine that I was immortal?" (Louis XIV; 1638 - 1715; a former king)
- "I have a long journey to take, and must bid the company farewell." (Sir Walter Raleigh; 1554 - 1618; a writer, poet and explorer)
- "Nothing matters. Nothing matters." (Louis B Mayer; 1884 - 1957; a film producer)
- "I have fought a good fight, I have finished my course, I have kept the faith." (Paul; an apostle of Jesus Christ; II Timothy 4:7;KJV)
- "It is finished." (Our Lord and Saviour, Jesus Christ; John 19: 30;KJV)

Last words: What could yours be?

Chapter 15

What happens after death?

I would imagine that this is the real million-dollar question — it is a very important but difficult question which needs answering but which no one can confidently answer. I doubt there is any single person who wouldn't like to know what happens after people die: Do they begin another life? Do they start another journey? Are they able to oversee the world of the living? Is there another existence, in an organised system similar to what obtains in the world of the living, in the great beyond? These, and possibly many more, are questions which almost every one of us would like definite and accurate answers to.

More so, I also believe more than just a few people would gladly give all or most of their material possessions in exchange for precise and accurate information as to what to expect after they die. I guess it is this uncertainty and mystery which surround what really happens after death that is partly responsible for why some people regard and treat death they way they do: often as a scary and unwelcome prospect and usually with some degree of awe and respect. Sometimes, even some of those who confidently claim to know what really happens after death, when at the brink of death, suddenly become unsure and are so quickly separated from their earlier assured confidences.

It is often said that death is a mystery and truly so, because in reality not many who have crossed the great beyond have been able to return to tell what really obtain at the other side. And so it would seem the only way of truly knowing what happens after death is to first die; but the irony is that once a person dies whatever knowledge they might come to as a result is of little or no relevance to him or her because by the time a person dies the knowledge of what happens after death serves him or her no benefit. Such people may get to know the answers to those questions we all wish we knew their correct answers but by then they couldn't do anything with such knowledge. For example, they couldn't make any amendments or be able to effect any changes, as a result, meaning that what they might then know would not be of any help to them. The only thing left for such people would be to simply brace themselves as they accept whatever they have coming to them or that would become their fate. Similarly, any such reliable firsthand knowledge acquired through death could not be useful to the living since such knowledge could not be made available to those who are still alive. It is not often that the dead come back to life; even in the rare cases when some dead do come back, the information they have is rather very limited and not sufficient to fully inform us about what happens after we die.

And so death, as it were, remains a mystery. Almost as life itself seems to be a mystery.

Is death a mystery though?

I suppose by now you probably would've realised that life is not really the mystery it seems to be. But what about death: is it really a mystery? Do we not have any clues as to what might obtain after death? Is it only by dying that we might have an idea about what happens after death?

I don't think so. Why? Because if that was to be the case then we could not really be expected to prepare for death and for what might lie beyond death — eternity. Without a sound and concrete basis we could not make any reliable and tangible preparation for eternity. Just as we couldn't reliably pack for a journey whose destination is unknown because with an unknown destination we would not know how to rightly prepare — what could be needed for the journey, what could be needed at the destination (e.g. appropriate clothing, currency, foods, etc.) and what or what not to do in order to be granted entry when we eventually get there. An unspecified destination could mean that we prepare wrongly, travel with things not needed where we are headed and would almost always result in surprises upon arrival, some of which might be unpleasant.

And so if we are expected to prepare for eternity, I will then expect that we would also be made available with the things needed for such preparations. Fortunately, this happens to be the case as God has provided us with sufficient information enough to assist us prepare for dying and for eternity. Although most of what happens after death are largely mysteries, we are not entirely bereft of information which might shed some light in that regard. We have been provided with an array of information about what happens after death just as we have reliably been provided with information about how we came into existence.

To start our quest — about what happens after we die — we shall go back to the beginning of life. The beginning of human existence holds some vital clues which might help us decode some of the apparent mysteries that surround death. In the beginning:

> And the Lord God formed man of the dust of the ground, and breathed into his nostrils the breath of life; and man became a living soul. (Genesis 2:7;KJV)

We are made up of two primary components: a body — formed from the dust of the ground — and a soul — as a result of the breath of life (God's breath). We are considered alive when those two components are active and functioning; death occurs when the latter component — soul — is separated from the body. When that separation takes place, what happens to the body is probably no mystery as I suppose we are all well aware that the body is usually disposed of in any of many ways — e.g. burials or cremations (with the resultant ash either scattered over a chosen location or subsequently buried underground). What however is largely unknown, and therefore could be regarded a mystery, is what happens to the departed soul or spirit. Here is the answer:

> Then shall the dust return to the earth as it was: and the spirit shall return unto God who gave it. (Ecclesiastes 12:7;KJV)

The first half of the above reference more or less confirms what is relatively common knowledge i.e. that the body is returned to the ground or dust from out of which it was made — the latter part now provides us with a concise information as to what happens to the soul or spirit when it is separated from the body at death — the soul returns to God. It seems rather obvious that since the body goes back to where it came from — dust — the soul can only be expected to also go back where it came from — to God. It would simply be unreasonable to believe otherwise. The human soul couldn't, for instance, simply vanish into thin air or simply cease to exist after being separated from the body at death: as a product of God's breath — the breath of life — the soul simply couldn't be expected to stop existing because God is never-dying; therefore anything from him, including his breath, could not be expected to die. And so it is more reasonable believing that our souls are also never-dying and continue to exist even after our body dies.

Now we know that when we die our souls return to our maker, God.

What happens after we die?

- The soul, having left the body, continues to exist; it also returns to God.

And then what?

A few significant and reliable clues abound as to what happens next, but we shall mainly explore some of those that have been made available to us by Jesus Christ:

> And before him shall be gathered all nations: and he shall separate them one from another, as a shepherd divideth his sheep from the goats: (Matthew 25:32;KJV)

And this:

> And many of them that sleep in the dust of the earth shall awake, some to everlasting life, and some to shame and everlasting contempt. (Daniel 12:2;KJV)

And so, it seems there would be a type of distinction or separation among all the souls which return to God — some souls would be classified as "sheep" and others as "goats"; some souls would enjoy everlasting life and others would endure shame and everlasting contempt. (The parable of the rich man and a certain man named Lazarus, in Luke 16:19 - 31, seems to further confirm this possibility of a dual and parallel existence in the great beyond; that there are two different possible states in which we could exist after death because Lazarus and the rich man found themselves in two different places after dying.)

Therefore, we now know one more thing which happens after we die:

- There would be a separation amongst souls — our souls would be congregated in two broad different groups.

But why a separation? And what could be its basis?

A few clues:

> For we must all appear before the judgement seat of Christ; that every one may receive the things done in his body, according to that he hath done, whether it be good or bad. (II Corinthians 5:10;KJV)

And also:

> So then every one of us shall give account of himself to God. (Romans 14:12;KJV)

And:

> And I saw a great white throne, and him that sat on it, from whose face the earth and the heaven fled away; and there was found no place for them.
> And I saw the dead, small and great, stand before God; and the books were opened: and another book was opened, which is the book of life: and the dead were judged out of those things which were written in the books, according to their works.
> (Revelation 20:11,12;KJV)

Based on the foregoing references, it would seem that this separation is necessitated for accountability sake — we have to be made accountable for what we have done with our lives. Sounds reasonable and fair because it wouldn't seem right that we wouldn't be held accountable for how we might've lived our lives. Or would it? We just couldn't choose to do anything we wanted without having to be responsible for our actions. Such a possibility would only make senseless, or even foolishness, of the various forms or systems of accountability with which we govern ourselves on this side of life: People are often held to account for the things they do here; our justice or judiciary systems, educational systems, employment and commercial systems, and more all tend to ensure that we assume responsibility for our various actions.

Similarly, it seems that we shall be separated based on how we have lived. Broadly-speaking, whether we did good or bad. Which also sounds reasonable and fair because it wouldn't have been fair had everyone been expected to share the same type of eternity regardless of how each person might've lived. Or would it? It also seems right and fair that what happens to us after we die is largely determined by what we did while alive, meaning that we are directly and primarily responsible for what would happen to us after we die. Fair, is it not?

(Please recall that I have often remarked that God made us with a freedom of choice; also that he to a greater extent allows us an independent expression and application of that freedom without always interfering with them.

Recall also that I remarked that God respects whatever he has ordained or decreed and would often allow them to run their full courses regardless of whether they pan out as he had intended or not. This might be why!: God plans to hold us individually responsible for our individual actions.)

Again, we now also know that after we die:

- We shall be made to account for how we lived.
- How we lived would in turn determine our classification.

(This is probably another motivation for us not to live just anyhow but to be circumspect, treating others how we would expect to be treated, doing good for the sake of goodness alone, and, more importantly, ensuring we establish and maintain a good and proper relationship with our maker, God, because how we treat God is also a necessity for which we are solely responsible for and for which we shall be held to account.)

After the separation, then what?

Some clues:

> And I saw a new heaven and a new earth: for the first heaven and the first earth were passed away; and there was no more sea.
>
> And I John saw the holy city, new Jerusalem, coming down from God out of heaven, prepared as a bride adorned for her husband.
>
> And I heard a great voice out of heaven saying, Behold, the tabernacle of God is with men, and he will dwell with them, and they shall be his people, and God himself shall be with them, and be their God.
>
> And God shall wipe away all tears from their eyes; and there shall be no more death, neither sorrow, nor crying, neither shall there be any more pain: for the former things are passed away.

> And he that sat upon the throne said, Behold, I make all things new. And he said unto me, Write: for these words are true and faithful. (Revelation 21:1-5;KJV)

More:

> But the fearful, and the unbelieving, and the abominable, and the murderers, and whoremongers, and sorcerers, and idolaters, and all liars, shall have their part in the lake which burneth with fire and brimstone: which is the second death. (Revelation 21:8;KJV)

And more:

> And in hell he lift up his eyes, being in torments, and seeth Abraham afar off, and Lazarus in his bosom.
>
> And he cried and said, Father Abraham, have mercy on me, and send Lazarus, that he may dip the tip of his finger in water, and cool my tongue; for I am tormented in this flame.
>
> But Abraham said, Son, remember that thou in thy lifetime receivedst thy good things, and likewise Lazarus evil things: but now he is comforted, and thou art tormented.
>
> And besides all this, between us and you there is a great gulf fixed: so that they which would pass from hence to you cannot; neither can they pass to us, that would come from thence.
>
> (Luke 16:23 – 26;KJV)

The foregoing references tend to imply that after the separation our souls would continue to exist — eternally — in one of two different states:

- Eternal bliss
- Eternal condemnation

I would imagine eternal bliss to be something similar to how Adam and Eve originally lived before they disobeyed God and became separated from him, although this time not with physical or natural bodies but as spirit beings — a stress-free and thoroughly enjoyable life! Eternal condemnation, on the other hand, would be a totally different scenario; going by the few clues provided in the Bible, I would suppose is better imagined than experienced — could best be described as doom!

And so, finally, even death and what happens afterwards seem to have also been demystified as we now have a few reliable hint as to what would happen after we die.

Epilogue

Life! — what a journey.

I should be saying to you: Welcome. Because we have come to the end of the journey. The journey itself — i.e. its main part — actually ended when we bade the world farewell — in Goodbye, World — and what followed was more like a preview of the next part — a sort of trailer for the sequel; a glimpse into the future. And so in a manner of speaking, the journey is now ended but it is not over. Life goes on… and goes on… and on. Life is a continuum — it never ends.

However, the next part of the journey is not as important as this first part until it is time for us to embark on that latter part of life's journey. And so focusing on this earlier part of the journey seems to be presently of more importance and relevance. More so, going by what we have discovered so far, it seems certain that if we handle this part of the journey properly then we would have set ourselves up to also experience the latter journey in the best possible ways and under the best of circumstances.

I suppose you would agree with me when I say: this journey has been an exciting one, or wouldn't you? It is possible we have now visited places we have never before visited or that we didn't even know existed. It is also possible we have tried out new things, seen new things and acquired new knowledge. Beautiful! Exciting! Scary (at times)! Interesting!

When we observed our last stopover, during which we had a brief comfort break, we tried to reflect on what could be — a new us and a brand new world — before we then proceeded to finish the journey. Subsequently, we discovered that there is a time to die; and when that time comes we would bid the world goodbye, after possibly having said our last words. We then briefly contemplated what those last words could be for us. Well, we have, again, come to another break — this time not a comfort one — which marks the end of the journey and after which we shall go our separate ways to continue a different but similar journey — this time the real one in the real world. We shall step out of this virtual adventure and enter into the real jungle — the jungle of life — where we are likely to encounter some or most of the things we encountered during this particular adventure: We may, for instance, encounter our old selves (for those who discovered and became their true and new selves during the journey) or we might yet become our true selves; we may come across people and see them differently from how we did previously; we may decide to do stock checks of our material possessions and might discover a few unwanted assets or properties accumulated possibly out of greed or wrong influences; we may get back to work and realise it isn't working for us and that we need something different or new, or we may resume our various businesses only to realise it would no longer be business as usual; we may get back home and realise we have made a mess of things, and we may see our spouses and children and realise we have failed them in many ways; and, finally, we may generally see life from a totally new and different perspective.

And so, as we disembark from this mini adventure and re-embark on the real journey, let us be certain that we would encounter ups and downs, fair weathers and adverse weathers, failures and successes, disappointments, betrayals, surprises (some of which might be pleasant, others of which might be unpleasant), kindness and cruelty, love and hate, and some more. But may we also remember some of the other things we encountered during this journey which could assist us in handling whatever might betide us on the real journey: Might we remember, for instance, that every circumstances we might encounter in life could have been permitted so as to help prepare us for opportunities that might be just around the various corners from such circumstances — may we endeavour to allow our circumstances make and not mar us; might we also remember, for instance, that our little deeds could lead to greater deeds, culminating in levels of greatness we could never have dreamt of — we may remember Joseph, the interpreter of dreams, who later became a ruler in the land of his captivity simply by interpreting dreams; might we also remember that in doing good we do ourselves good, we stand to gain more from our various acts of kindness and goodness than those who are at the receiving end of our actions — may we also remember that one good turn although should deserve another is not always reciprocated with another good turn, but that shouldn't deter us from doing good all the same; might we also remember that we are unique and so instead of trying to be like others should strive to be better versions of ourselves; might we remember YOLO — you only live once — and so endeavour to give that one and only shot our best; might we also remember that once the journey — the real one — comes to an end we would be needing death's ferry service in order to cross over to the other side of life, and once we cross over there would be no coming back meaning we should endeavour to finish every business on this side which can be finished when they can be finished and avoid putting away for a later time what can be done now; and also in doing all that we can, might we remember to ensure we do all things right and to the best of our abilities because in the end we shall be made to account for all we have done and our deeds would be compensated accordingly; finally, might we also remember that it is up to us to decide what type of eternal existence we want — eternal bliss or eternal condemnation — so that we might choose rightly how the latter and eternal part of our journeys would be.

I believe that life shouldn't be taken for granted: Life is a gift which we didn't ask for and therefore must be appreciated; it is a privilege not a right and therefore an opportunity which must be capitalised. Gifts are often received with gratitude and the gift of life shouldn't be an exception: We ought to be grateful for having being brought into existence; our gratitude should then cause us to treat our maker — God Almighty — with reverence, respect and love; it should also cause us to treat other human beings and the rest of creation with love, respect, acceptance, patience and grace because by respecting God's creation we also show him respect. To truly respect we first need to love; in loving, we live for we are made in love, because of love and for love — to love is to live and to truly live is to love. (Perhaps another mystery solved.)

The journey has long been over, we were only observing an end break — for catch-ups and goodbyes — during which we recounted a few of our experiences during the journey and some of what we might expect going forward. Even this end break is now over and we must part ways. As I pick up my luggage to go my separate way let me quickly say: It was nice journeying with you, sad we have to now say goodbye and go our different ways but have a good life. Make the real journey worth this journey and who knows, we might even meet again. Adieus!

Bibliography

1. YouVersion.com. **The Holy Bible** version 6.3.2 King James Version (KJV), Crown Copyright in United Kingdom.
2. Livescience.com. Eric R. Olson, Life's Little Mysteries Contributor. **Why Are 250 Million Sperm Cells Released During Sex**. January 24th, 2013 (accessed October, 2015).
3. Wikipedia.org. **Rosa Parks**. (Accessed October, 2015).
4. Nelson Mandela. 1995, **Long Walk to Freedom**. Macdonald Purnell.
5. Newworldencyclopedia.org. **Cogito ergo sum**. (Accessed October, 2015. Last modified on June 3rd, 2013).
6. Thinkexist.com. **Adolf Hitler Quotes**. (Accessed October, 2015).
7. Nationalgeographic.com. **Genographic Project/ The Human Journey: Migration Routes**. (Accessed December, 2015).
8. Realhistoryww.com. **Ancient Man and His First Civilizations (China-2)**. (Accessed December, 2015).
9. Historyworld.net. **History of Slavery**. (Accessed November, 2015).
10. Wikipedia.org. **History of Colonialism**. (Accessed November, 2015).
11. Wikipedia.org. **The Holocaust**. (Accessed November, 2015).
12. Wikipedia.org. **Genocides in History**. (Accessed November, 2015).
13. Wikipedia.org. **Armenian Genocide**. (Accessed November, 2015).
14. Wikipedia.org. **Rwandan Genocide**. (Accessed November, 2015).
15. Oxforddictionaries.com.
16. Google.com.
17. Thefreedictionary.com.
18. Wikipedia.org. **Jesus (name)**. (Accessed November, 2015).
19. BBC.co.uk. Dr Sophie Lunn-Rockliffe. **Christianity and the Roman Empire**. Last updated February 17th, 2011. (Accessed November, 2015).
20. Wikipedia.org. **Constantine the Great and Christianity**. (Accessed November, 2015).

21. Realtruth.org. David C. Pack. **The True Origin of Christmas**. (Accessed November, 2015).
22. CARM.org. Matt Slick. **What are the Origins of Christmas?**
23. Christiananswers.net. **Where did "Easter" get its name?**
24. Ancient-origins.net. April Holloway. **The Ancient Pagan Origins of Easter**. April 20th, 2014.
25. Wikipedia.org. **God (word)**. (Accessed November, 2015).
26. Wikipedia.org. **Tetragrammaton**. (Accessed November, 2015).
27. Wikipedia.org. **Jehovah**. (Accessed November, 2015).
28. Crystalinks.com. **Nubia**.
29. Wikipedia.org. **Nubia**. (Accessed December, 2015).
30. Wikipedia.org. **Natural Resource**. (Accessed December, 2015).
31. ITV.com. **What is Sarah's Law?** Last updated December 23rd, 2013. (Accessed December, 2015).
32. Phrases.org.uk. Gary Martin. **The meaning and origin of the expression : A fool and his money are soon parted.**
33. Phrases.org.uk. Gary Martin. **Famous Last words**.
34. Corsinet.com. Brian Candy. **Last Words**.

Lightning Source UK Ltd.
Milton Keynes UK
UKHW040747170420
361781UK00008B/55